To Liam

Lest We Forget

A Time of Innocence

Hope you enjoy this stroll
down memory lane
Regards
Martin

By

Martin Coffey

ISBN: 978-1-905451-54-8

A CIP catalogue for this book is available from the National Library.

This book was published in cooperation with
Choice Publishing & Book Services Ltd, Drogheda, Co Louth, Ireland
Tel: 041 9841551 Email: info@choicepublishing.ie
www.choicepublishing.ie

Dedication

I dedicate this book to the memory of my brother Joe Coffey and to my parents Bernard and Mary Coffey.

I would like to thank the following people for their support and encouragement, most of whom have had some kind of input or influence on me during the writing of this book either through photographs, stories or words of encouragement.

Mary Renehan, Gerry Walsh, the Coffey family, Angela O'Neill, Gracie and Maggie Doyle, the Burke family, Larry Maher, the Educational Company of Ireland, the Cabra History and Folklore Group, Choice Publishing and Book Services Ltd, and to my children Mark, Sinead, Elaine, Martin, Ailis and Joseph,

A special thank you to the early settlers of Cabra West for their determination to succeed.

Contents

Introduction

These pages are filled with my own personal memories and thoughts of what it was like growing up in a large family in the North Dublin suburb of Cabra West. I lived there in the same house with my family for nineteen years. So much of my early childhood and adult life was moulded and shaped by my family and the people of this area. I have tried to tell of events and people as seen through the eyes of a young boy moving through different stages of his life. The inclusion of so many photographs may prove relevant in providing a greater understanding of the overall story.

I have included some portion of my parent's background as a lead in to the main story. I feel it is necessary to show where they were coming from in order to understand why they decided to make the move to Cabra West. I was born on Halloween, Thursday October 31st 1951. My parents already had seven other children. I had two older sisters and five older brothers. Seven more children were to follow, two younger brothers, and five younger sisters. There is almost two years between each of my mother's children.

I first attended a school run by nuns. I then graduated to primary school proper and had a relatively easy time there. I later went on to a Technical School to prepare for a possible trade on leaving the Irish Educational System. It was here that I was told I was too stupid to make anything of my life. In recent years I graduated from N.U.I Maynooth with a Double Honours Degree in English Literature and Celtic Studies.

Ever since my graduation from university I have wanted to combine my newly acquired knowledge of the English Language with the historical research I have carried out on my family history over a thirty year period. I decided to start with my own memory of growing up in a large family and to describe what life was like having to survive amidst fifteen siblings and several neighbours' children.

One of the most impressive qualities that my parents had was that of charity towards each and every person that came to them for help. They never turned anyone away from their door. My mother instilled a great love of reading into most of us. She was rarely if ever without a book to read. My father was selling newspapers at ten years of age. Both of my parents had exceptionally good handwriting for two people that came from very deprived backgrounds. My father's family had lived in the Monto area of Dublin for over 150 years.

Growing up as a child in Cabra West during the 1950's and 1960's almost seems like something from a long forgotten dream. The classrooms of the schools I attended are practically empty of young boys today. Once they were bursting with forty plus children in each room. Poverty as it was then amongst the newly arrived tenants has ceased to exist. Very few people if any pay rent to Dublin Corporation because now the tenant is either buying or has bought their house outright. Almost every home has a car and telephone. Something that was unheard of all those years ago. Most of the first generation of pioneers into Cabra West have gone and are now replaced by subsequent generations.

Bernard Coffey (left) with his twin brothers

Chapter 1

My Parents Background

My father's name is Bernard Joseph Coffey. He was born in 1912 in a place that no longer exists on any street map of Dublin, Purdon Street. My mother is Mary Agnes Burke. She was born in 1919 in the Rotunda Hospital. My parent's were reared in the infamous Monto red light district of Dublin city. An area once recognised as the most socially deprived area of the then British Empire, an area over run with prostitution. As a young girl my mother would often call many of the prostitutes from that area by the name of Auntie, not because they were related to her but simply because they were often used as babysitters by her mother when she was a small child.

My mother slept in the same bed as some of these girls and played outside on the street with their children. As a young boy my father would often run errands for the girls or take care of a cabby's horse while he and his fare paid a visit to the girls. It was all part and parcel of normal life for young children growing up in this area of the city. In the 1920's Frank Duff and the Legion of Mary campaigned to clean up the Monto area of prostitution. This meant that some of the women had no place to live. It was suggested to them that they could go into one of the Magdalene homes run by the nuns.

Monto Girl asleep in street

According to my father some of the girls had originally come from these institutions and had no intention of ever going back to them. Many of the girls were alcoholics. At that time my mother's parents lived in number eleven Elliott Place. This street was right in the heart of the Monto and regularly frequented by the girls. One prostitute named Ginger Kate took to sleeping on the floor at the top of the stairs outside the room where my mother's family lived. Eventually my grandmother allowed her to sleep in their room on the floor underneath her kitchen table. During the daytime Ginger Kate would keep an eye on my mother and her sisters. Young married couples too often ended up sleeping under their parent's kitchen table because they had nowhere else to live. Nothing came easy to the people of this era. Everyone struggled on an almost even footing.

Each night Ginger Kate went off to ply her trade. She kept her supply of beer hidden in a metal bathtub under my grandmother's bed. Other times she hid her drink in the slop bucket or rubbish bin. Some of the prostitutes took to hiding their drink in the shores by the sides of the road. The people of the Monto area seldom if ever referred to these women as prostitutes. They were known as the girls. Some years earlier a London serial killer by the name of Jack the Ripper had murdered several prostitutes and the girls of the Monto area were very much aware of similar dangers that lurked in every shadowy laneway of their area.

Johnnie Carroll & Mary Agnes Burke

When the authorities decided to close down the business of prostitution in the Monto they received great support from the people of the locality. The people of the area despised those that lived off the earnings of the girls but never despised the girls. One time the police raided the area looking for illegal drink. They came to my grandmother's flat because they knew that Kate stayed there. My mother and her friend were playing on the floor near the bed where Kate had her drink hidden. To my grandmother's relief the children said nothing to the authorities about the hoard of drink under the bed.

Similar to young children growing up in the early years of Cabra West my parent's grew up in their neighbourhood knowing no different. Within the confines of the area in which they lived my family struggled to survive amongst the deprivation that surrounded them. Before moving to Cabra West my parents had lived in a one room flat at the top of a tenement house in Gardiner Street close to Summerhill. They had four children at that time, two girls and two boys. Next-door to them there was a pub on the corner of Parnell Street and Gardiner Street. The pub had a small yard at the rear where the men went to the toilet. There was just one snag with this arrangement however. The pub had no toilet for women. Instead the women would use the hallway of the tenement house next door where my parents lived, as an area to relieve themselves. The stench of stale urine would cling to the very walls and stairs of the building.

Tumbling Tenements

Each morning my mother would have to pour hot water and disinfectant onto the hallway floor and scrub it out to try and get rid of the smell. My mother had four young children that she had to manage up and down several flights of stairs. She had to battle through this stench every morning. How could anyone think that it was okay to urinate in the hallway of someone else's house?

Unemployment was everywhere in the New Free State. Those unfortunates who found themselves in this situation held out little hope for change. If a man was lucky he might get a days work on the docks loading or unloading a ship. One time when my parents lived in Summerhill my father was without a job. He went to the priest in the Pro-Cathedral and asked for help from the Society of Saint Vincent de Paul. This was a catholic organisation set up to help the poor and destitute of the city in times of need. My mother had three little babies and another one on the way. She was only twenty five years old and had no food to feed her children.

In those desperate times going to the Vincent's was a last resort. It was considered by some as being next door to begging in the streets. The Priest would personally call on a family who requested assistance and assess their situation. When my mother was told to expect the priest she immediately cleaned and tidied their flat. When the priest finally called and saw the neatness of the flat he told my mother that he did not see them as being in need.

9

Mary Agnes Burke (right) & friends 1935

At times my family would often move home on a regular basis, sometimes staying within the same tenement building. Everybody was always on the lookout for a bigger room or maybe two rooms or perhaps somewhere that was cheaper to rent. Each tenement had only one toilet between several families. This was situated outside in the garden at the rear of the building. The stench from these old toilets was overpowering but what could the people do? The landlords and their agents did nothing to help. It seemed that all they were interested in was money. Some people kept a potty shoved in under their bed so they would not have to go out into the cold night to relief themselves. Others had a bucket placed in the corner of the room for the family to use.

On more than one occasion the contents of the potty or bucket was just emptied out of the window into the yard or street below. God help anyone walking along the footpath when this happened. The people in the tenements saw nothing wrong with this method of waste disposal. My mother's family kept their slop bucket out on the landing. In wintertime the tenements were always freezing cold, there was no central heating, and in fact some families had no heating of any kind. It was not unusual to see families breaking up their furniture to burn on the fire.

10

Top floor flat in Gardiner Street

While most people tried their best to keep their own part of the house clean the landlords did next to nothing to help. There was no electricity or running water indoors. A gaslight lit each room. And of course every house had its own particular ghost. Whoever was sent down to the yard in the dark of night to fill up the kettle for the father's breakfast was always aware of the ghostly figure standing in the corner of the hallway or yard.

Bits of Work

My father worked as a conductor on the buses for a while in the 1940's. He worked out of Clontarf Bus Station. The buses were in competition with each other back then. They could often be seen racing each other along the seafront from Clontarf into the city centre vying for business from waiting passengers. He also secured Christmas work in the postal sorting office in Sheriff Street. This was only a temporary job and later on he secured a full-time job as a labourer working on the construction of the roadway and houses in Stillorgan in south county Dublin.

When he was working on the road construction in Stillorgan my father bought a bicycle on hire purchase so that he could get to work each morning and save money on bus fares. He would give one of the other workers a lift on the crossbar of the bike and charge him a fare that was cheaper than the bus.

11

Rafter's Pawnshop in Gardiner Street

This helped to pay off the cost of the bicycle. He also managed to rent out a plot of land near Leopardstown, not too far from where he worked. He planted and grew his own vegetables here. He tended this vegetable plot every Saturday after work and would bring home some of his produce for the Sunday dinner. My father eventually ended up working as a bank porter for the rest of his working life. When he started working in the bank he gave up the plot. A lot of ex-servicemen secured jobs as porters in the bank. It almost became an extension of their army service. My father had joined the British Army in the early 1930's.

At that time there was very little work available in Dublin for young men of his age. Some of them opted to join the British Army more out of a sense of survival rather than loyalty to King or Country. My father was stationed in Malta for most of his service years. Having served with the army for the best part of eight years he eventually returned to Dublin to marry my mother in 1938. They were married in the side chapel of the Pro Cathedral.

I think my father originally started working as a bank porter in what today is generally known as the Irish Permanent Building Society on the corner of Abbey Street and O'Connell Street. This building was originally a bank. He found coins in the old vault that were melted together from the fires of the 1916 uprising. One day the Bank Manager told my father that for security reasons both he and his family were to move into the small flat situated on top of the bank building.

Private Bernard Coffey 1930

My father went and told my mother of the decision made by the bank manager. The new flat was rent free but had as many steps and stairs as nearby Nelson's Pillar. True to form my mother refused to move out of her own little one roomed flat. She was not going to jeopardise her independence to please any bank manager. As a result my father moved into the bank on his own leaving behind my mother with their young children. He was afraid of losing his job and felt he had no choice when the bank authorities told him to jump. My mother thought otherwise. My grandmother shamed him in public into moving back with my mother. At first my mother hesitated in taking him back to teach him a lesson. He still retained his job. My father looked on his job in the bank as being safe and secure. It gave him a feeling of pride having full time employment and being able to support his family without the aid of government or church handouts.

In Ireland of that time some people, like my father, felt that they were still under the thumb of British Colonialism and had a type of fear of their betters. In certain large companies and stores the management team had to be addressed by mister or sir along with their first or last name. "Excuse me please Mister John" or "Excuse me please Mister Smith" was considered the correct way to address one's betters. You always answered with "yes sir or no sir". My father always referred to his boss in the bank as 'manager'.

Paddy Coffey in a tenement flat

It was always "Yes manager, no manager, and six bags full manager". My father also worked for a while in the Hibernian Bank in Dorset Street. He then worked in a bank near the cattle market in Prussia Street. Eventually he moved to a branch of the Hibernian Bank in Camden Street. He once wore a top hat and tails when he worked in the Bank. He was never offered any compensation for being shunted from one place to another. Because of a road accident in the 1970's involving a hit and run my father was forced into early retirement.

His old bicycle that had served him so faithfully for years was stolen from the scene of the accident near Queen Street. What kind of mentality exists in some people to justify them stealing from the scene of an accident? My father cycled everywhere and my mother mostly walked to any place she wanted to go to. As a child my mother would often walk up into Drumcondra and pick blackberries.

The bus service then only went as far as the Cat and Cage pub. If you wanted to travel any further there was an ass and cart service that went out to Portrane Hospital. My mother had previously worked for Mitchell's Rosary Bead Factory at the back of the Dandy Garage in Waterford Street. The first news reader on Irish television, Charles Mitchell belonged to this family.

Horse & Cart Man

The factory is long gone now. When World War II broke out in 1939 my father wanted to re-enlist along with some of his relations and old army buddies. My mother basically told him that if he re-joined their marriage was over where she was concerned. He had a choice to make. He never joined up. Perhaps my mother should have stood by him but how would she have coped with a young family if he were killed in action?

Everything was so convenient for people that lived in the city centre. Shops and hospitals were all within easy walking distance of where they lived. The main problem for most families was overcrowding. The crumbling tenements were bulging at the seams with families. The government of the new Free State decided on a plan of major expansion into the surrounding countryside. In the old Cabra area they would build 1,950 houses to accommodate the overspill of families from the slums of the city. This was a major undertaking for the new government of the time. Construction of the housing estate began in 1938. The Cabra West area of Dublin was considered by most city dwellers as being beyond the Pale.

It was unexplored territory for most of them. Anything beyond Phibsborough was alien to most northside city dwellers. The vast majority of these people had no reason to venture so far out into the countryside. The area within the North Circular Road was their safe zone.

Maggie & James Doyle with their children in the Monto 1901

This ran from the Five Lamps on the North Strand to the Phoenix Park gates. There was nothing of interest beyond this area for the people from the Monto.

As a young teenage girl of sixteen years my mother was often warned not to venture into Irishtown now known as Ringsend. She was told that the people there were different than her own kind. When a boy from Irishtown would leave her home after a dance she would never allow him to go any further than Moran's Hotel in Talbot Street. She was always afraid that her mother would find out about him and put a stop to her dancing. She would often go to an area of Irishtown called the Shelly Bank near the ESB power station to watch the boys swimming.

The Tans v The I.R.A.

As a child my father remembered sitting in a barbershop in Talbot Street as the Black and Tans chased down the street after members of the I.R.A. The two cars were speeding along with bullets whizzing through the air similar to a scene from an American mobster film. As my father jumped off the barber's chair for a better look at the action the shop window shattered with a crash as a hail of bullets hit it. The barber grabbed my father and threw the two of them onto the shop floor. They lay on the floor covered in shards of glass and clumps of shaven hair.

Archie & Aggie Coffey 1940's he returned to Dublin

My father also remembered a time when Moran's Hotel in Talbot Street was under siege by British troops firing at the Republicans inside. He would often point out bullet holes on the outside wall of the hotel. Phil Shanahan's pub on the corner of Foley Street and Corporation Street was a safe house for I.R.A. men on the run and for their secret meetings. My father often stood outside the doorway and ran errands for the men inside.

My father's Aunt Kate hid a Black and Tan soldier in her flat to prevent him from being killed. When things quietened down he sneaked out and made his way back to his barracks. He returned some years later looking to thank her for what she did for him. Unfortunately she had died by that time. Her husband had been shot by British troops in 1916. During WWII her son was taken captive by the Japanese in Burma where he was forced to work on the famous Bridge over the River Kwai. My father had originally written a letter to him from Malta encouraging him to join the army for a better life. These were certainly strange times for most people. At this particular time he remembered seeing three or four men dressed in overcoats and hats pulled low over their eyes go into a pub on the corner of Gloucester Place and Railway Street. This was Hyne's public house.

Baby Vera Coffey

Suddenly there was a great rush by the men inside to get out of the place. My father then heard voices being raised followed by several shots being fired. As the men in the coats came out of the pub my father looked in and saw someone lying on the floor in a pool of blood. Word quickly spread that the man was an informer for the British and that Collin's boys had done a job on him. This is a reference of course to Michael Collins and his squad of hit men, famous for their resistance to the British Crown. The man shot dead was John Ryan; he was a brother to Becky Cooper, one of the most renowned madams in the Monto area. Anyone named as a spy or informer spent a lot of time looking over their shoulder. Eventually a knock would come to the door or a shadow would creep up on them. No one was safe.

My mother's Aunt Mary and her family were great supporters of the Republican Movement. When my mother was a young girl Countess Markevitz had her pose for a pencil sketch at a Republican fund raising event in the Mansion House. Her Aunt Mary and the Countess were great friends. Mary had once been a school teacher. Unfortunately the sketch later disappeared when her Aunt Mary died. As a child my mother was brought to all the Republican funerals and fund raising events held in Dublin. The Aunt Mary always encouraged my mother in her education and gave what help she could to ensure that my mother could read and write.

Barney Doyle with Bernard and Billy Coffey

My father and mother spoke fondly of Becky Cooper and May Oblong, two well-known madams from the Monto area. They both had a great affection for all of the girls that they knew from their childhood days. This is how life was for my parents growing up and marrying in the slums of Dublin. It would appear that my parents were doomed to live out their days with a large litter of endless children arriving one on top of the other in squalid tenement conditions. It seemed that for most people life held out little or no hope of change.

News soon began to spread around the neighbourhood that the housing department of Dublin Corporation was in the process of allocating houses in the suburbs to potential families. Unknown to my father my mother wrote a letter into the housing office asking to be placed on their housing list for consideration. Everyday she kept an eye out along the street for the postman. She had only confided in her mother about the letter.

Perhaps life was going to give them a chance after all. They could have a garden for the children to play in and running water indoors as well as electric light. They could even have their own indoor toilet. Was it possible? Most everyone in the neighbourhood was filled with excitement at the prospect of getting a house.

Chrissie, Billy and Vera Coffey 1944

Chapter 2

Into the West

One day a letter arrived at the tenement flat addressed to my father. Official letters were always addressed to the man of the home. It was from the housing section of Dublin Corporation. When he arrived home my mother excitedly showed him the letter. "Dear Mister Coffey…" it began. After reading the letter my father threw it onto the fire. "I'm not moving out to the bloody country for any shagging Corporation" he said. My parents were being offered the key to a house in Cabra West. They were instructed to bring the letter with them to the Corporation Offices in Jervis Street.

My mother quickly snatched the flaming letter out of the fire. She said to my father "Well if you want to stay here you can stay here on your own because me and the kids are going." My father realised that he had bitten off more than he could chew. My mother was a very strong-minded woman when it came to her family. She saw this move as a chance to break free from the filth and squalor of the tenements. It was basically a new start for her and my Dad. It was an opportunity to have a house they could call their own. The following day she headed off to the housing office with the scorched letter in her hand. The office was mainly filled with women eager to avail of the offer of a new house regardless of where it was.

Noel & Archie Coffey 1948

As usual there was rarely a man in sight when it came to dealing with the Corporation. As my mother stood in the queue with a determined look on her face an older woman stepped back and engaged my mother in conversation about the scorched letter.

My mother upped and told her the whole story. She had a captive audience with the rest of the crowd that had gathered in the office listening in. For most of them this was too good a story to miss. There was plenty of input from the audience. "The bastard, yer right misses leave him where he is." "God love yeh misses you've the patience of a saint." What great support she received from her comrades in arms. They were probably relating to their own situation as they hurled abuse about my father across the room. The woman who stood back and spoke to my mother was Mrs Katie O'Brien. It just so happened that my family moved in next door to the O'Brien family in Cabra West and remained great neighbours with them for over fifty years.

In the 1940's there had been a massive migration of poor families from city centre slum dwellings to the newly built housing estates that began dotting the outer suburbs of Dublin. As well as Cabra West there was Crumlin, Drimnagh, Ballyfermot and Finglas. The Catholic hierarchy at that time had insisted that each family had to have at least three children in order to qualify for a house.

Brendan Coffey 1951

What a terrible burden to place on the shoulders of a people that were already struggling to make ends meet with what little they had. The Church did little to help in raring the children. It still insisted however on shoving out the collection plate every Sunday. Another mouth to feed was a big price to pay for what was on offer. My mother was just thankful for the chance to move her family out of the slum dwellings of the tenements. One neighbouring family of ours eventually had twenty-three children and they were still confined to a two bedroomed house. With the amount of open space available in Cabra West Dublin Corporation could easily have built large three and four bedroomed houses

Everything from schools to shops was easier to get to in the city centre. Originally there was very little infrastructure in place to accommodate the move from city to rural living. There was no official bus service running into the heart of Cabra West. The number twelve buses ran from O'Connell Street to Quarry Road in Cabra East. For some families this could mean a good walk of a mile or so to get home, depending on where they were housed. If for instance someone lived on Ventry Road it was at least a good mile to travel. They might have to walk across mud and fields in the dark of night to get home. Not every road had properly paved streets or footpaths. Street lighting was also a scarce commodity in some areas.

Killala Road 1952

My parents eventually had fifteen children. They had eight boys and seven girls. They were never upgraded to a bigger house. The most children we had living in the house at any one time was probably about eleven or twelve. We were really entitled to three houses. In later years one family in the area was actually given two houses side-by-side that they turned into one big house. I have no idea as to how they managed it.

We never had anything other than two bedrooms between us all. The new people of Cabra West were no different to the people of many other Corporation or Council estates throughout the country on moving into their new houses for the first time. Change takes time and is often resented. It is not always possible to pick your neighbours and that too can come as a challenge to some families.

The early people of Cabra West were pioneering people who took on the challenges of a new era. They came, they saw and they conquered, but most of all they endured. In a style similar to the early pioneers of the American Wild West my father pushed his young family and belongings to the wilds of Cabra West on a handcart. They eventually arrived at Killala Road as dusk settled. The Indians came later. My family would live at this new address for the best part of sixty years. Eventually each family settled into their own way of living and coping in this new environment.

Martin Coffey 1952

Most everyone was willing to help their neighbour out with the loan of a cup of sugar for their tea or a lump of burning coal to light a fire with. As the excitement of the move gradually receded the people of Cabra West appeared to be content with their lot.

The first winter that the people of Cabra West encountered was miserly, cold and bitter. It was still considered the war years and everything was rationed out. Nothing was in plentiful supply. Most families resorted to breaking up their household furniture to burn a fire for heating and cooking. Beautiful kitchen dressers, chairs and antique sideboards brought out from the city were smashed up and thrown onto the flames. Overcoats were used on the beds for blankets. They became known as blankets with pockets.

On one particular Sunday morning the new tenants awoke to find themselves covered under a blanket of snow. People had to use shovels to dig their way through the snow in an attempt to get to Mass. The shovels had to be brought into the little tin church on Fassaugh Avenue to stop others from stealing them. About two or three years after moving into their new homes the people of Cabra West were finally allocated a cast iron bath to each house.

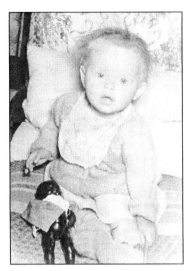
Anne Coffey 1954

The baths were left in the front gardens for quite a long time until arrangements could be made to have them properly installed. Originally the houses had no railings or walls and horses would freely roam about from garden to garden peeking in through the parlour windows.

There were no shore covers in place at any of the houses because my eldest brother Billy fell down the shore in our back garden on our families first evening of arrival. With great excitement at the idea of a new house with a garden he ran through the house and out into the back yard. He went straight down into the shore and stuck his leg into it. The next-door neighbours came and pulled him out.

When the gas was originally run into the houses metal piping was in short supply. The tubular frames from bicycles were welded together in place of proper piping to run the gas through. In the early 1980's the gas company were called out to investigate a gas leak outside our house. They had to dig up the footpath of the house next door and that is when my father saw the gasmen taking up old pipes made from bicycle frames. Perhaps Cabra West back then was a reflection of the condition of the new Free State as it too struggled to come to terms with its new identity.

The Coffey's & John Burke 1956

Surviving the Move

My parent's never really looked on themselves as a working class family. I don't think anyone in our neighbourhood ever had the time to give themselves any kind of label like that. It was simply a case of very few people having any kind of work. Therefore they did not really qualify as working class in the proper sense of the term. Because my father had permanent work George Orwell may well have referred to us as middle working class. People never had the time or the inclination to stop and ask themselves to what class they belonged.

Almost everyone was struggling in their own way to keep themselves and their families above the poverty line. It was as if our neighbourhood had become one big extended family struggling for survival. We were all paddling in the one mud boat called poverty. It never really mattered whose child you were or to what house you belonged. Almost everybody supported each other as best they could. Neighbours were neighbours no matter what. My mother often took other children into our house to feed them, especially if their own mother was ill. Other times it was because the children were just neglected by their own families. Nobody was ever turned away from our house.

Billy & Brendan Coffey

I remember an older homeless man that would call to our house. He would sit at the end of our stairs and my mother would bring him out a cup of tea and maybe a slice of bread. On the odd occasion he would sit at our dinner table and have a bite to eat. Most times he preferred to sit at the end of the stairs. Sometimes a homeless couple would call to our house.

Supposedly the new tenants in Cabra West were advised to get used to living in the downstairs area first before moving upstairs. This was a reference to the situation they experienced while living on one landing in the tenements. My father quickly became accustomed to the idea of moving out of the city centre. He hired out a handcart from a place in Granby Lane. Most everyone that moved to Cabra West had used the same mode of transport. The government offered no assistance. People were basically left to their own devices when it came to moving their belongings out to the suburbs.

With great excitement and trepidation they moved in their droves hopeful for a better life for them and their children. With what little they had my parents struggled financially for years to feed, and cloth their large family of eight boys and seven girls. Even though money was scarce I don't ever remember going hungry.

Martin, Bernard & Anne Coffey

Our neighbour Granny O'Brien had a daughter Molly who had worked in North Williams Street School for a number of years. For quite some time Molly brought home some of the leftover sandwiches and milk from the school and handed them into my mother to feed us on. On instructions from her mother Molly would cut the sandwiches in half so that there were some left for the next day. I remember my mother going without to ensure that we all had enough to eat and that my father had his dinner on the table.

My mother spent over eight years of her life pregnant. Most of her children were born in the Rotunda Hospital in Dublin's city centre and the rest were born at home. My brother Brendan was born in the kitchen while my mother was preparing the dinner. It was not unusual for the women of this area to deliver each other's babies. When young unmarried girls in the area became pregnant they either married straightaway or were sent off to England to put the child up for adoption. Some girls never returned. It was often put out that they had gone to England to work but everyone knew. It was all based on a fear of shame. If you were over twenty one and unmarried people would think that there was something wrong with you and you were then labelled as an Old Spinster or an Ould Bachelor.

Mary, Tony and Catherine Coffey with their Mum

Chapter 3

Our House

We are the Coffey's and we lived in number 36 Killala Road in Cabra West. This is where my parents would raise fifteen children as best they could. Our family was no different to most families in our neighbourhood. We put margarine on our bread just like everyone else. We could not afford butter any more than the rest of the families around us. Sometimes we had to make do with putting dripping on our bread. This was fat that had solidified from cooked meat. Sometimes it was sold in the shops for cooking purposes. Most of what we ate on our bread came from my mother's own cooking.

Whatever you refused to eat someone else would swallow. When food was in short supply in the house our dog always looked kind of nervous. We were always told that if we were hungry enough we would eat anything. We often had cow's tongue for Sunday dinner. We would then have cow's tongue sandwiches for our tea. Anything with meat on it was eaten. We didn't have very much in our house. Everything was very basic, nothing fancy or uppity and rarely if ever did we have anything that was new.

29

Portmarnock 1956

I think all of the furniture was second-hand, either bought or handed on from someone or other. There was a blue and white kitchen dresser that stood against the wall next to the kitchen door. This was probably brought out from town on the handcart when my parents first came to Cabra West. My mother kept a metal breadbin in the bottom part it. The breadbin as far as I know was a present that my parents had received on their wedding day so very long ago.

One of the drawers in the kitchen dresser had a collection of knives and forks and other odd bits of cutlery. There were some small egg spoons known as the twelve apostles that my parent's had from their wedding. Nothing seemed to match. I don't remember what the other drawer held. I remember the drawers had a distinct smell, not a fragrance just a smell. In some drawer or other my mother always kept a tin box stuffed with an assortment of buttons and old zips.

On the wall beside the dresser was the one and only electrical outlet or socket in the entire house. My father had it jammed tight with all sorts of double adaptors that had electric leads stretching in all directions. There were no electric sockets upstairs or in the hallway. Everything electrical started and finished from that one point in the kitchen. Each room in the house had an electric light bulb. We had a table and very few chairs but certainly not enough to seat us all at the one time. I have a vague recollection of someone sitting on an upturned tea chest.

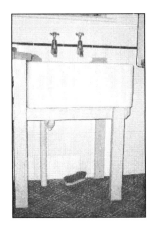

The Old Kitchen Sink

The Kitchen

In the kitchen there was a corner press with a shelf in the middle. Most people knocked this press down to make more room. When my father was knocking our one down the head slipped off the hammer he was using and struck him on the knee. My mother had told him it was loose but he chose to ignore her warning. Our kitchen had a gas cooker and a very large ceramic sink. There was also a small porch partitioned off the kitchen. This is where my mother would usually hang the Christmas puddings. Any pots and pans that we had were stored out there also.

Our first dog slept in this porch for a while. There was an alcove under the stairs that was approached from the kitchen. It had a wooden door and the gas meter was also housed in under the stairs. Most people kept their coal and turf there and we called it the Coalhole. In later years my mother had a curtain put up to divide the kitchen area from the living area. That is how it was done in the tenement rooms. A curtain was hung across the room to divide it in two, cutting off the sleeping area from the rest of the room. My father made a stool from some scraps of timber he had. Most of us had to stand at the table when eating our meals. Our main fireplace was made of black cast-iron. There was a small hob on both sides of the firebox where a kettle of water could be boiled. Some people used the hobs for cooking on.

Anne Coffey

My brother Brendan used them for melting plastic toy soldiers on. We loved the colourful flames that they gave off when he threw them into the fire. If there was no money for the gas then the dinner was cooked over the fire. Above the hobs there were two small black oven doors with knobs on them. I have no recollection of our oven ever being used for anything other than drying out chestnuts for my older brothers to play conkers with.

Everything from shoes to hair was burned in the fire. Each morning when the fireplace was being cleaned out all of the cinders from the half burned coal was kept to one side in a bucket. My mother would throw potato skins on the cinders and then she would empty the tea leafs from the night before onto that. When the fire was roaring hot my mother would put a couple of old shoes into the fire and then load on the contents of the bucket. The fire would hiss and spit and appear to us to go out. We all moaned and complained in harmony at the loss of heat. After about a half hour however everyone would have to move away from the fire because of the intense heat caused by the mix my mother had thrown on. Big red and white blotches would break out on your legs from sitting too near the blazing fire. For some reason we called these blotches ABC's. It was always a dangerous thing to sit too near the fire wearing your wellies. You could get a really nasty burn from the hot rubber if it touched the skin on your leg. The best thing of all about the roaring fire was being able to make toast from its heat. Making toast on the fire was the best of all things to do.

Mary and Bernard Coffey

You would stick a dinner fork into a piece of bread and hold it in front of the fire. You would have to wrap a cloth around the hand that you held the fork with to stop yourself from being burned. A big blob of margarine was put on the bread and it would ooze off and run down your chin as you took your first bite of freshly toasted batch loaf. Some things were certainly worth waiting for.

During the winter months my mother would gather us all like little chickens around the kitchen fire as dark shadows danced across the ceiling. Each and every little face would glow red from the flaming fire. We huddled even closer together as our mother began telling us tales of haunted tenement buildings and ghostly shapes she had witnessed in the darkness of a rain soaked night. We were absolutely terrified out of our wits. As the outside light of day faded fast we huddled even closer still.

A sudden knock at the hall door would send us all into a terrified frenzy of fear. Our little hearts would pump with fright as we screamed "Oh Mammy". As the faded echo of our screams resounded in the kitchen I was usually shoved out into the darkness and away from the heat of the fire to investigate who the strange caller was. Perhaps it was Dracula or Frankenstein calling in for a cup of tea. The experience of walking down the dark hallway was a terrifying ordeal. It was usually some kid wanting one of us to go out to play.

Martin & Anne Coffey 1955

The Parlour

Very few families ever used their parlour as a third bedroom. In the early years my parents never did. Like most of our neighbours our parlour was kept for visitors to sit in. The door was usually kept locked and the room was rarely used. Most any visitors that came to our house were related to us so they were brought into the kitchen. It was like a secret room that we could only glance into through the outside window. Even then we had to climb onto the window ledge to see in. Our parlour was like a secret garden to us. It was full of mystery and bewilderment. It had a full cast-iron fireplace with a mantle piece over it. There was also a sideboard under which my father kept two swords that he had brought home with him from his time in the British Army. He later gave them to a butcher who made knives from them.

There were also two antique dogs sitting on the dresser. There was a great big bunch of large keys for all of the doors in the house. One time two detectives called to the house and were brought into the parlour. My older brother Noel and his friend had saved a girl from drowning at the seaside and the detectives called to our house to get a statement from Noel. I think that happened back in the late 1950's. Some years later Noel bumped into this particular friend while living in Colchester in England.

Brendan & Anne Coffey

The Toilet

Most all of the houses in our area were built of redbrick. The same redbrick was used on Saint Finbarr's national school and also on the local shops. The vast majority of houses in Cabra West were built to the same plan. They were built with two bedrooms and a toilet upstairs and a kitchen and parlour downstairs. The toilet had a bath and a cast iron water cistern that was placed high up on the wall from which hung a chain for flushing the toilet. The toilet seat was made from wood.

Other houses however had three bedrooms upstairs and a toilet downstairs next to the kitchen. Thankfully our toilet was upstairs next to the bedrooms. We never had fancy coloured soft tissue toilet paper and our shirt tails were very definitely not to be used. Yesterday's daily newspaper was always in great demand in our toilet. We would peruse the cartoon section and crossword puzzle before condemning it to a faith worse than death. Sometimes my father would bring home toilet paper from the bank. This was the posh stuff that came in little green boxes with a slit at the top where the paper could peek out. Some types of paper could leave you with paper-cuts across your cheeks. Others however had a shiny surface that resulted in your swipe slipping and sliding all over the place.

Willie Kavanagh, Martin Coffey & Girls

Because we had so many in our family it never mattered what time of day or night you sat in the toilet because somebody was sure to come banging on the door demanding that you hurry up and let them in. On Sunday mornings my father used the bathroom for shaving and singing. He would belt out the words of all his old army songs as he washed and shaved. "Bless them all; bless them all, the long and the short and the tall...." On it would go until he had finished his shave. Others used the bathroom as a reading room. In cases of emergency we used the shore in the backyard as an extra toilet. This was situated just outside the backdoor.

Toilet Trouble

When my brother Joseph was a small boy he was unable to reach up to the toilet bowl to pee. My father came up with an ingenious solution to the problem. He brought home an empty wooden tomato crate which he turned upside down and nailed a piece of lino onto it. By standing on this new contraption Joseph could easily reach up and do his business. Late one night my father had a few drinks on him and had to use the toilet. He forgot about the new contraption and stumbled over the upturned tomato box. As he was falling he put out his hand to save himself. His hand and arm went straight into the toilet bowl. His broken arm was in a sling for some time.

Vera & Anne Coffey in the back garden

Our Bedrooms

We only had two bedrooms in our house. The boys all slept in the same one, usually the back bedroom. This room measured approximately ten foot square. There were six or seven of us in this room at any one time. We were like Sardines stuffed into one little tin. I remember when there were three beds, a wardrobe and a baby's cot in the back bedroom. Every night the windows and bedroom door were shut tight to keep out the cold. Any fresh air was soon replaced with the smell of dirty socks, farts, belching, coughing and cigarette smoke. We were always afraid to touch anyone else in the bed in case you got a kick or an elbow for doing so. All night long there was a constant tug of war with the blankets, sheets and overcoats.

When I was sixteen I was still sharing a bed with two of my brothers and one of them was older than me. I slept at the foot of the bed and they slept at the top. Eventually in the late 1960's my mother bought two sets of bunk beds. One set for the boy's room and one set for the girls. Most nights my eldest brother Billy would sit up in his bed smoking in the dark. Once the light was turned out you were not allowed to talk. I would lie there watching the light from the cigarette blaze up with each puff and imagine it to be a train in a dark tunnel. Most every other house in the neighbourhood had similar sleeping arrangements.

Mary and Martin Coffey 1957

One time my brother Noel brought me to see a film in Finbarr's Hall called Abbott and Costello meets the Mummy. At that time I was about six or seven years old and had to sleep in the cot. There was no room anywhere else for me to sleep. That night I had a bad dream about the film so Noel took me into the bed with him on one side of me and Brendan on the other. Finbarr's school often had film shows in the school hall. They were mostly cowboy films. They were shown on Saturday mornings and Sunday afternoons.

My parents slept in the front bedroom with the girls and whatever baby was around. Rarely had they a quiet moment to themselves. In 1954 however they did manage to take a holiday on their own to the Isle of Mann. My younger sister Mary was born the following year. Sometimes our sleeping arrangements were changed around and you could find yourself sleeping in the wrong bedroom. On a whim my mother would re-arrange the bedrooms while we were all at school. In later years as my younger sisters became teenagers my parents used the front parlour as their bedroom. It was easier for my father to fall into when he had a few drinks taken. For a while we had a bed settee in the parlour. This was usually used when we had family home from England or one of us was sick. My father would move it into the kitchen so my mother could keep an eye on us.

Vera & Aggie Coffey with baby Mary in her pram 1955

No matter who was sick everyone would jump under the bedcovers and sit beside them while having their dinner. It really didn't matter much to us where we slept. In the front bedroom we had a bit more room than in the backroom. I had to hang my guitar on the wall over our bed because there was nowhere else for it. Sometimes during a winters night my father would light the gas fire in the front bedroom to heat the place up for us. We would huddle close together like new born mice for extra heat from each other.

One time my father brought home metal hot water bottles. Well that's what he called them. There was the usual squabble amongst us as to who should get one first. If two of us could agree to lie back to back then we could both get an equal share of the bottle by placing it in between the two of us. Other times we would pour warm water into a glass lemonade bottle and take that to bed with us. We had to make sure that the water was never boiling in case the bottle smashed from the heat. Our bedrooms were freezing cold but we just had to undress as quickly as we could and jump in under the bedsheets. There was no sense in standing about on the equally cold floor moaning and complaining. On most occasions we wore our socks in bed. We had no underwear back then so all the little parts of our anatomy suffered equally from the cold. I liked to sleep wrapped up in a ball with my two knees firmly up against my chest. A little bit like one of the old bodies they find in a bog from ancient times.

Our cousins the Kane Family

It is sometimes difficult to put into words how cold we were back then. Usually the only source of heat was from the fire in the kitchen. The rest of the house was freezing cold. Once you moved away from the fire the cold would almost instantly cling like a wet rag to your little frame. When I look at old black and white films of Victorian England and see the people walking about their house in fur coats and smoking jackets I can relate to how they feel. Most of them appear to get over-dressed when going to bed with their night caps, gowns and bed socks. Maybe we should have done the same.

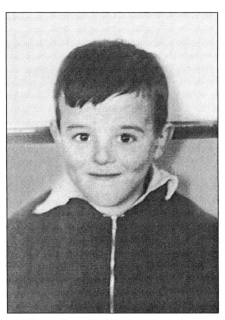
Brendan Coffey school photo

Chapter 4

Ghost Stories

As a very young girl my mother had seen her uncle Jim kneeling at the end of her bed holding his rosary beads in his hand. My mother went and told her aunt Mary what she had seen. It was soon discovered that her uncle Jim had died in hospital at about the time my mother had seen him in her bedroom. My mother told me that she had often experienced situations similar to this. She would sometimes read tea leafs for girls on our road. At a homecoming party for a neighbour that had arrived home from service in the British Army my mother was asked to read his tea leaves. He got more in his tea than he bargained for when she later told him to make up his mind about the woman in England or his wife. The family later moved to England. My father and my Uncle Ned Burke were clearing out a house on the Cabra Road when a ghostly figure appeared in the garage. They had just finished setting fire to an old mattress when the figure appeared inside the garage door. They both thought that maybe the ghost had money hidden in the old mattress they had set fire to and was haunting them for it.

Martin Coffey with Aileen O'Brien

Making Room

Like the old woman that lived in the shoe large families needed plenty of room to move about. There was no money available to build on an extension to our house. My father decided to knock down the back porch in our kitchen to give us some extra room. This gave us a little more room to spread ourselves around the dinner table. We had an assortment of odd chairs and wooden stools to sit on.

One time we even had a car seat for an armchair. One day I was sitting on it and caught the fingers of my two hands underneath the back rail. I was trapped. All I had to do to release myself was to lean forward but I was in too much pain to think straight so I just screamed. My granny Burke was sitting at the kitchen table talking to my mother. She reached over without saying a word to me or interrupting the flow of conversation with my mother and clattered me on the back of the head. This course of action sent me and the car seat flying forward. Problem solved. She was the only grandparent I ever new. Because I was so young I never really knew her or much about her life. Like my mother she seemed quiet and private. As a young child she was sent to a home in Tipperary run by Nuns.

The Coffey's 1954

Two of my brothers once locked my grandmother into my father's tool shed. She chased after them with the intention of giving them a good old beating for getting up to no good. They escaped through the hen house and out through the little opening into the chicken run. They then locked the shed door and ran off.

Dinner and Tea

At dinnertime my father and mother sat at the head of our table. My father sat on the right hand side and my mother sat beside him. There was a pecking order in place. We were more or less placed around the table in order of our ages. The eldest sat nearest to our parents and the smaller ones stood around the rest of the table. If there were any other chairs or stools it was usually the smallest ones who were given them, as they were unable to reach up to the table. The rest had to stand and chew. My father usually arrived home from work at about six o'clock in the evening. We never said grace before meals or the rosary in our house. I suppose we were too hungry to wait. Hesitation was always a dangerous thing at the dinner table. To do so meant that you weren't hungry and could be seen by others as a signal to help themselves from your plate.

Coffey's Back yard 1952

The Disappearing Dinner

Once a dinner was placed on the table you were expected to eat it straightaway and with no hesitation. I remember one Sunday we were all seated around our dinner table while my mother was standing over by the kitchen sink. I looked at my dinner and saw something that I always hated. Steeped peas were something that I could never take to and here they were sitting on my plate next to a couple of boiled potatoes and a strip of cow's tongue. I must have passed a remark about them because Brendan suggested to me that I should leave the dinner table and tell my mother about them. Of course I listened to him and approached my mother about my distaste for what was on the plate. When I returned to the dinner table my plate was wiped clean. Every last morsel was gone. The strangest thing is that nobody seemed to know what happened to my dinner. I never complained again or left the table while I had food on my plate.

The Angelus Bells

Each evening when the Angelus bell rang out from the nearby church my mother would give the order to pour the tea. My father would soon arrive home from work with his bicycle and we would all help to retrieve any goods he had tied to the carrier on the back of his bike.

Vera Coffey

He always brought home the evening and morning newspapers. My father wore a soft cap and a big heavy woollen overcoat to ward off the elements. He also wore bicycle clips on his trousers to stop them from becoming entangled in the bicycle chain. When he came indoors he would always smell of cold air.

Sister in England

Sometimes during the day when the Angelus Bells rang out my mother would stop what she was doing and say a prayer that my sister Vera would do well in England. Vera had moved to England to study as a nurse. Like a lot of young girls of that period she had worked in Williams and Woods Jam Factory at the back of Bolton Street School. They also produced chocolate sweets. Vera was never allowed to bring any chocolate home to us. She could however eat all she wanted on the premises.

Every now and then a large parcel wrapped in brown paper or a cardboard box would arrive on our doorstep from England. Vera would very often send home what she could to help out my mother. The boxes were usually filled with second-hand clothes and books.

Chrissie Coffey

The twine and wrapping was ripped and thrown to one side as we fought each other to lay claim on the contents. If something didn't fit we tried our best to make it fit. One time I ended up going to Finbarr's school wearing a blazer that was a size too big for me.

It had a crest on the breast pocket from some school or college in England. I didn't mind because my friends were mad jealous of it. What must my teacher have thought to himself when he saw it? Strangely enough he never made any comment on it. He most probably knew of course how I came to have it. Some Friday nights my father would try and ring Vera in England from a local phone box. The operator would instruct him to have the exact amount of three shillings and five pennies ready to insert into the coin slot. There were very few public phone boxes in our area and people would have to queue up outside to use them.

Entertainment

We had no television back then. On Sunday nights my father would produce two pairs of boxing gloves and he would have my brothers sparring each other with the gloves on. It was good entertainment for those not involved. I never tried it. My mother would sit listening to the radio as her knitting needles clickity clacked together in the background.

Coffey Relations from the Monto

One time my father brought home a plastic kit and put it together with the help of a tube of glue. He painted it in various colours and before us stood an airfix model of a Tower of London Beefeater. He followed on some weeks later with various other models. We were amazed at what he had created. My brother Brendan made a model of Joan of Arc. For years these two figures stood inside my mother's glass cabinet. Another time he showed us how to make a house from matchsticks glued side by side.

Sometimes my father would set up a game of push penny. We played this game on the kitchen table. We used two combs and three coins, two large and one small. It was usually two pennies for the players and a ha'penny for the ball. The goalposts were made using old coat buttons. The players used the combs to shove the pennies at the ha'penny like football players running and kicking a ball. The first player to score three goals was the winner. We would set up a little league and name ourselves after whatever English football team we wanted. We usually played this game on a Sunday night after we all had our school homework done. We called homework our ecker. One time my father bought a record player and we would often sit around the kitchen listening to the 1958 music of the film South Pacific. Mitzi Gaynor sang about washing that man out of her hair. In 1960 we had Elvis Presley singing Wooden Heart from his film G.I. Blues.

Martin Coffey in the back garden 1953

This was his fifth film and was made after his two year tour of army duty in Germany. We also had country and western music by Marty Robbins singing about El Paso and his white sports coat with its pink carnation.

Unwanted Guests

There were two types of insects that lived with us. One of these we called a hopper. The beds were full of hoppers. These were the little insects that would suck on your blood as you slept. They were most often fat and reddish brown, full to the gills with fresh blood. They could hop a great height. Some Saturday morning's my brother and I would lift up the rim of the mattress and find literally dozens of fat hoppers soundly sleeping after gorging themselves on our blood throughout the night. On the word go he would start at one end and I would start at the other.

We would try to outdo each other to see which of us could crush most hoppers between our thumbnails. There was a loud click as each hopper was squashed into oblivion. Blood would splatter up onto the backs of our hands and sometimes up into our faces. My brother Brendan always won the race because he was better at cheating than I was. In school almost every boy wore a white shirt and their collars would be speckled with blood from the hoppers bites. I think that the Hoppers could talk to each other. They would wait until we were asleep before feasting on our blood, then someone gave the go-ahead for the all clear. We called the other insect a flea.

June & Mary Coffey

DDT

Fleas were always found in your hair. Today they are called nits. They could jump from one head to another. Sometimes another type of flea would jump off our dog. Maybe they were really hoppers too. Fleas were quite small and white. They were removed from your hair by using a special fine comb. My mother put liquid DDT into our hair to kill them off. She also used a DDT powder to kill the hoppers in the beds. The mattress, blankets, sheets, pillows and pillowcases were covered in a fine white dust of DDT powder. When you lay down to sleep at night a fine white mist rose up from the bed and settled over you as you dozed off. This would often result in making us cough and bark for a while until the DDT quietly settled into our lungs.

Even our dog was turned white when the powder was shook all over him. Brendan and I were usually sent over to a chemist shop in Thomas Street for the powder and liquid. My job was to keep watch at the shop door and look out for anyone we knew that might be passing by. We didn't want anyone to know what we were buying. In recent times a European Law banned the use of DDT. It was also used extensively in the American - Vietnam War to destroy vast areas covered by trees and foliage. It most probably killed off several thousand animals and humans as well.

John & Anne Burke with her Piggy

By 1972 most countries had banned the use of DDT for agricultural purposes. In America it was shown that DDT could possibly cause cancer in humans. Liquid DDT was put in our hair. You could smell it a mile away. Every family in the area had hoppers and fleas. This was very evident by the state of the shirt collars on the boys I went to school with. On Monday morning we always wore the same shirt that we had worn to Mass the day before. This one shirt would have to last us for the rest of the week. The shirt collars of the boys sitting in front of me in class were always speckled red from the hoppers they had feasting on them the night before. We were never sent home with a note to our mothers advising them to clean our heads of the infestation of lice.

It didn't seem to matter how many children a family had most of them were still only given a two bedroomed house. All of the houses backed onto each other. Each house had a front and back garden. Some houses had a wall at the front and others had railings instead. It really depended on what road you lived on. I suppose for people that never had a garden before anything was welcome, wall or rail.

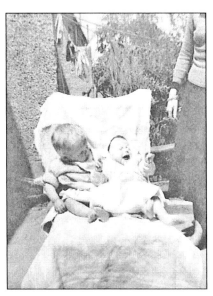
Martin Coffey & Kathleen Cullivan

A house with a wall always seemed more posh to those that lived in a house with railings. It was always a challenge to the bigger boys and girls to see if they could walk tightrope fashion along the length of the railings dividing one house from another. A loss of concentration resulted in a whole lot of pain if you slipped and fell onto the railings.

Gardens

The back gardens of the houses were more like a wilderness. They were certainly not landscaped. Some corner houses had very little back garden as they were shaped like a triangle. Lengths of wire divided the gardens. At times my father grew vegetables in a part of our back garden. He also rented a plot across the road from Glasnevin Cemetery. He arrived there one Saturday morning to find that all of his produce had been stolen. He gave it up as a lost cause.

Some people put up a kind of makeshift shed in their garden. My father put up a shed and a chicken run. There was a door leading from the shed into where the hens laid their eggs. He kept his motorbike and tools in the shed. We also had a makeshift pigeon loft in our backyard. My father later turned it into a bicycle shed. He had meat hooks hanging from the roof and the front wheels of the bicycles were hung from these.

Bernard & Anne Coffey 1955

The people of Cabra West may not have been totally self-sufficient but at least some of them tried as best they could. Mrs O'Brien from next door had my father take down the dividing wire between our gardens. She wanted us to have plenty of room to run about in. She seemingly enjoyed the noise and laughter she could hear us making. She never complained as we ran through the open doors of her house and back in through our own.

Our house was originally destined to be a rent office. Above and below the parlour windows can be seen the holes that were meant to house iron bars. Our road has a large roundabout on it. It was commonly called the field or the roundabout. It was just an area of wilderness surrounded by a small wall. It was originally earmarked as a football field with a wire fence surrounding it. The Corporation must have run out of funds because they never finished this job. Maybe they just ran out.

Dublin Zoo

Chapter 5
The Zoo

To give my mother a rest from the stress of her large family most Sundays after dinner we were all herded off to the Cabra Grand picture house out of the way. The odd Sunday in the summer my father would bring a gang of us up to the Phoenix Park to see the zoo. We were never actually brought into the zoo because it was too expensive for so many children. We were allowed to walk around the outside perimeter fence and gaze through the wire at whatever animals we could see. They looked better fed than we were. Their meals were certainly more nutritious and the monkeys were given more fruit to eat than we ever had. We only saw large quantities of fruit at Halloween.

Farm Animals

A lot of people in Cabra West raised chickens and some even had a goat. Well our next-door neighbour had one. They let it sleep upstairs with the children. Another family kept a monkey in their attic. We had a hen named Mother Carey. She would make her way onto the kitchen table looking for crumbs. My father would buy little yellow chicks and raise them to full birds.

Grandfather William Coffey

They would arrive home in a brown cardboard box on the back carrier of his bicycle. We loved it when the box was opened and we saw the little yellow chicks all fluffy and chirping. There was so many of them stuffed inside the little box. Little did they know the fate that awaited them when they grew older. One of our next-door neighbours worked in the butchering business. They thought nothing of cutting off a chicken's head and letting the body run around the garden until it dropped dead to the ground. My father killed one of our hens one time and chased my older brothers with it. They ran and screamed about the house.

Seaside Rock

One neighbour in particular that I knew of slept in her parlour beside the window. She sold broken seaside rock to the children in the neighbourhood. She kept the rock under her mattress and would pull out a handful in exchange for a penny any time someone would knock on her parlour window. It seemed to me that she spent most of her time in the bed. This is almost beyond belief because every bed in the area was alive and walking with hoppers and all sorts of smells and God only knows what else. Every road had someone that sold something or other. Another family on our road had a shop van for a while and others sold small bundles of sticks for lighting the fire with. People did what they had to do to survive.

Anne & Martin Coffey

Landlocked

The housing estate of Cabra West was surrounded and land-locked on all sides by various institutions and man-made objects. It almost appears as if these institutions were purposely placed. They were almost like a daily reminder to the people living within their boundaries that they were under the constant and watchful eye of their betters. On the opposite side of the Phoenix Park wall sitting in absolute luxury was the President of Ireland. The majority of people in Cabra West lived in absolute poverty. These were opposite ends of the social spectrum in the recently formed Irish Free State, except there was nothing much free for the people of Cabra West.

 The Royal Canal and the railway line hemmed Cabra West in on the north. To the south were the Grangegorman Lunatic Asylum and Mc Kee army barracks. To the east was Glasnevin Cemetery; the largest of its kind in the country and slightly further across was Mountjoy Gaol. To the west was Saint Joseph's Christian Brothers School and Saint Catherine's Nun's Convent. The nearby Phoenix park wall also acted as a barrier. So no matter what direction you took there was a constant reminder of being hemmed in.

Noel Coffey & his Mum 1952

Other families in the area had even less than we had. We were lucky in that our father had a permanent job with the bank. Most of the men in the area were unemployed and some even unemployable. Being poor and unemployed put a lot of unnecessary strain on family life. Those who could took the boat to England and looked for work there. Some of them even started up a second family over there. It was never openly mentioned that couples had separated or split up. On a rare occasion money would somehow find its way home to the first family.

Once in a while some of the men would even return home for a holiday but would always go back to their second family. It was often said of such husbands that he was 'working across the water'. You could always tell the women whose husbands were absent from the home. Early in the morning, possibly from around six or seven o'clock, you could see some of these women cleaning their windows or sweeping down the pathway outside of their houses. Some of them even went so far as to sweep the roadway outside their house. Their houses were shining inside and out. Not a spot of dust could be seen. These women would spend hours rubbing and polishing the brasses on their front door.

Coffey Kids

They always had a smell of carbolic soap and disinfectant on their clothes. There was nothing in place to support these women as they struggled to come to terms with their situation of being left alone to raise a family. Sometimes you would see them hurrying along in their slippers heading off to the priest's house. The priest became a sort of surrogate husband who they waited on hand and foot feeding him his breakfast, dinner and tea. Times and society were hard on these poor unfortunate women. There was no such thing as deserted wives allowance back then.

I suppose that the priest would have paid them something for the work they did. Other women took to cleaning the church everyday. In later years I asked my mother why it was that these women did these sorts of things and she said that they were venting their sexual frustrations. They were most likely venting their anger at the misplaced husband. These women always wore their aprons under their coats and had their headscarves knotted tightly under their chins. Their noses were blue from the cold and their fingers were frozen to the bone. Their homes and children were spotlessly clean. They never seemed to smile however. In fact nobody ever seemed to smile. Perhaps the second wife was doing enough smiling for the both of them.

Bernard Coffey 3rd from right

Poverty

Some families gave little or no attention to their homes or children. One boy I went to school with had fallen out of the top bedroom window of his house as a young child. He damaged his skull so much that he had a metal plate inserted into it. He was slow to learn in school. He always had dark green snots running out of his nose. My teacher referred to him as the Lord Mayor of Rathoath Road. The boy would pick bread up from the ground that other boys that thrown away in the schoolyard. His mother would make bread pudding to feed them with. I would later wonder why the social services or the church did not intervene to help such families. In school we were given buns on Wednesday and jam on Friday.

One particular friend of mine was very often left out in the rain by his stepmother. Sometimes his older brother would be with him standing at the side of another neighbour's house in the pouring rain. My mother would send me out to bring them into our house out of the weather. It was a regular occurrence every Friday for him to steal a steak and kidney pie from a nearby shop and hide it in the hedge in our garden until the way was clear for him to retrieve it for eating. There were several other boys I knew of in similar situations. I have no memory of anyone ever being turned away from our house. There were other families who lived in total denial of their circumstances, afraid to admit that they had fallen on hard times and too proud to look for help from a neighbour.

Butcher's window with pig's feet and tripe.

It seemed to me as if they considered themselves a cut above everyone else. They would go into city centre to borrow from the moneylenders. They would not want people in the neighbourhood to know their business. Others like my mother didn't care too much who saw the Jew Man coming to her door. My mother eventually became a kind of collecting agent for the Jew man from Mary Street, unpaid I might add. People would quietly slip their weekly payments or excuses to my mother. She would then pass them on to the Jew Man. The only people who knew their business were themselves, my mother and the Jew man. Even in their most desperate hours these people still insisted on holding onto their pride. Pride never put food onto the table or a roof over one's head.

There were many families that survived solely on the money borrowed in this way. My mother often had to rely on the Providence Cheques. She took us along with the Providence Cheques to the Blackrock clothes shop in Chatham Street to dress us. I think Mister Talbot from lower Carnlough Road collected payment each week for the Providence. Sometimes on a Sunday morning my mother would send me around to his house with the money. I have no idea what kind of interest my mother would have paid on any loans she had secured from the Jew man or anyone else, probably as much as twenty to twenty five percent. I have no recollection of other moneylenders in our area although there most likely was.

Chapter 6

Pay Up or Else

With the war years coming to a close practically everyone lived from hand to mouth. One course open to people was to shop in one of the second-hand clothes markets around town. There was the open air Hill Market in Cumberland Street and the indoor Ivy market on Francis Street. One could dress out an entire family from these markets quite cheaply provided they were not too fussy about what clothes they wore or who wore them beforehand. My mother very often brought us to the indoor Ivy Market to dress us, especially coming up to Christmas. Some of these market places were dirty and unkempt and often had a smell of damp clothes.

In the early days of moving to Cabra West my mother would still do most of her shopping in Nelly Gorman's in the Monto area of Dublin. Gorman's had most customers buying off the slate. At that time the new shops in Cabra West didn't have that same service on offer. Most every family lived off some slate or other. There was no other way. We always had someone or other calling to our house at the weekend for money. Granny Groves would call on Friday evening for her newspaper money. The milkman usually called around that time too. Another collector that called to our house was Frank from Sloan's. He called on Saturday morning and always seemed to be in good humour. Frank was a great man for the football.

The Coffey's

Another man that came to our house on Saturday morning was Mister Indian Teak. Well that's what we called him. He would always say that some of our furniture looked like it was made from Indian Teak. He would let himself into the house and shout up the stairs for us to get up out of bed. My brothers would always shout back some words of abuse at him.

The Coal Man

Another caller to the house was the black-faced coalman. He would most often arrive in a great big lorry. Along with his helper they would carry big heavy bags of black coal on their shoulders and as they walked through our kitchen they would leave a trail of coal dust on the floor. The coalman always seemed to arrive when my mother was in town. My older brothers were warned by my mother to count every bag that came through the house before handing over any money.

There was always a chance that someone or other would try to diddle you out of what little you had. Some coal men went around with a horse and cart doing their deliveries. These were independent coalmen who worked for themselves. They would buy a certain amount of coal from the main coal yard and sell it on in smaller quantities.

Noel Coffey

The Gas Man

The gasman would appear very officious when he would call. Unlike the coalman he was always dressed in a suit with collar and tie. We would all stand around the kitchen table as he emptied the coins from the gas meter onto the table. The gasman always had a particular way of counting out the shilling coins. He would spread them out flat on the tabletop and slide them one by one off the table into his hand.

Silently he counted out the money to himself. He would arrange the coins into neat little pillars of maybe ten coins or so to each pile. The money would then disappear into little paper bags. For some strange reason, which I could never figure out, he would always leave a little bunch of one-shilling coins on the table for my mother.

Some people used to rob their own gas meter. They would say that someone had broken into the house and stolen the money. I know it happened but not as often as some people claimed. These people were so desperate and destitute that in many cases they had no other option open to them. They had to feed their family. How was a mother to explain to her hungry young children that they had no money?

Billy Coffey

The Milk Man

In the early days of growing up in Cabra West there was a milkman that went around in a roman style chariot. There were two milk churns on each side of him as he stood in between holding the reins. When he came onto our road I would jump onto the chariot and help him with his deliveries. There was always a smell of horse from him. My job was to run from door to door and collect empty milk jugs for him to fill up.

There was no mention back then of pasteurisation or the like. Milk was milk no matter what shape or size it came in. Another horse drawn milkman was John from the Merville Dairies in Finglas. I think that he was the last of his kind. The Norton's that lived across the road from us always worked with him.

The Chimney Sweep

Not too unlike the coalman the Sweep was covered from head to toe in black soot. He would cover the opening of the fireplace with a big piece of rag that had a hole in the middle. My mother would have us place old newspapers across the floor. The sweep would assemble his rods and carefully put the first one with the brush on it through the hole in the rag. We all thought this was great fun.

Bernard, Brendan, Billy & Noel

We would all run out of the house to see who could be first to spot the brush as it emerged from the chimney top. There was great excitement as we ran into the house screaming that it had come out. When he was finished he would leave a big bag of soot behind him. This too, like the horse manure went on our garden. Sometimes my mother would have us clean our teeth with a bit of soot. Later on she would buy a small round tin of Colgate toothpaste for us. The chimney sweep usually came to our house at Christmas time. It was said to be lucky to have a chimney sweep at a wedding.

The Slop Man

In most areas of Cabra West there was always someone or other who collected slop. They might come around the roads on a horse and cart or they might have a designated place at the side of their house where people could empty their slops. The slop usually consisted of potato skins and cabbage leafs or leftover food. The slop was fed to pigs to fatten them up. Whacker was the name of the man that mainly came around on a horse and cart. At the end of our road Mister Mc Keever had a cart at the side of his house where we emptied our slop. There was always a horrible smell from it. It was certainly very unhygienic to have it so near to the little side window that opened into their kitchen. Mister Mc Keever always looked like a cowboy.

Neighbours & Coffey's

To me he was a very tall man He wore a cowboy hat and tanned boots like the cattlemen wore. He reminds me of the father from the television series Bonanza. Every Halloween the Mc Keever's gave out loads of goodies to the children from our road. Mrs Mc Keever was always very lady like in her manner. By giving so much to the children of the neighbourhood at Halloween they were probably saying 'thank you for all of your slop'.

Hand to Mouth

Nearly everyone that came to our house to collect money turned the key in our hall door and let themselves in. Some people kept their hall door key on a piece of string tied to the doorknocker and had it hanging inside through the letterbox. Nobody actually had a door key hidden because everyone knew where they were placed. People had little or nothing to fear from burglars because there was nothing worth stealing in a house in Cabra West.

Most of the people in our neighbourhood were constantly robbing Peter to pay Paul with interest so they had no interest in robbing each other. They were all living from hand to mouth, one day at a time. In the summer months most people left their front door wide open during the daytime and only closed it at night time.

Martin Coffey

A Good Neighbour

We had mostly good neighbours. My parent's knew most of the people in our area because they had grown up with them and had all moved out to Cabra in or around the same time. I think my father's best friend was Jemmy Hayes. He lived across the road from us. My brother Billy would often send me over to the Hayes' house for a swap of cowboy books. Mister Hayes was usually sitting at their table with a big mug of tea in front of him and chewing on a crust of bread. I have no memory of him having any teeth. His wife was a soft woman with a great big heart. She would always give me a big chunk of bread smothered in jam.

During one of the major Dublin bread strikes my father and his friend Jemmy Hayes cycled to Drogheda, a round trip of over sixty miles in one day, to buy bread. When they arrived in Drogheda they approached the main bread shop in the town. My father said that the owner was a Protestant and refused to sell them any bread. He also said that one of the girls made eyes at Jemmy Hayes and she gave him the nod to meet her at the back of the bakery. Unknown to the owner she filled up both their pillowcases with bread and sent them on their way back to Dublin. When they arrived home my father made sure to share what they had with some of our neighbours.

Some of the Coffey's

That's just the way it was back then. During other bread strikes my mother would send some of us to queue outside Boland's bread shop on Fassaugh Avenue.

Summer Evenings

 At the beginning of our school holidays a lot of young boys had their heads shaven. This was to rid them of head lice. One family near us had to shave their girl's hair. They had great big scabs on their heads. The girls had to wear headscarves but we all knew what was up with them. Everyone made fun of them. The holidays were always a great time for us kids. It seems as if the sun rose extra early and stayed bright in the sky until late into the night. The long evenings were great because we were allowed stay out until dark.

The girls would all set up shop with empty boxes and tin cans for sale. These were exchanged for pieces of chaney, which was broken pieces of crockery and delph. The chaney was broken into sizes similar to the coinage of the day such as pennies, ha'pennies and two-shilling pieces. Really small pieces could be used as farthings. The last shop I remember taking the original farthing was Boland's bread shop on Fassaugh Avenue. The farthing had a swallow on the front. 'Buy away, buy away new shop open, ham, jam anything you want mam.'

Anne Coffey & her Dad

There were four farthings in a penny. Sometimes dock leafs were sold as rashers. The dock leaf was also used for rubbing on a nettle sting. A long length of old rope came in handy for the girls to play skipping with. Two girls would take a hold onto each end of the rope and start turning it. A long line of girls would soon gather and each one would take a turn at running and skipping into and out of the turning rope. Sometimes the rope could be long enough that the girls could double it over and have two ropes turning in opposite directions. On an odd occasion I remember some of the mothers joining in with the skipping.

It was a great sight to see a herd of cattle or sheep being driven by drovers along the roadways of Cabra West. It was like something out of a Wild West film. The drovers would travel by rail from the midlands with their herd and take them over Broombridge onto the Rathoath Road and straight down to the cattle market in Prussia Street. Young boys could often make some money by helping out the drovers. At times they might be given a cattle stick for their efforts. One of my brothers sometimes brought home a can of fresh milk from the market. Sometimes he might be lucky and be given a cattle-stick to take home as well.

Mary Agnes Coffey

Mothers Shopping

Years ago a lot of people did their family shopping everyday. Nobody had a fridge to store perishable foods in. Meat had to be bought on a daily basis. Bottles of milk were kept in a bucket of cold water during the hot weather or placed outside the back door during the winter months. There was a type of daily ritual that the women of the area carried out. At around ten o'clock every morning of the week the mother's of the neighbourhood could be seen gathering around the local shops on Fassaugh Avenue. Gossip, stories and local news were all exchanged at this time.

They would go to the same shops in a particular order. The butcher shop belonging to Mister Hunt might be first and then off to Beechener's vegetable shop. After that they went for their bread into Boland's bakery and into the Capitol Stores for milk and margarine. One time my mother left my baby brother Joseph in his pram outside the butcher's shop and went home without him. It was a while before she realised where he was. Sometimes we were sent to a bakery in Thomas Street for stale bread. This bread was cheaper than what was normally bought in a bakery shop. My mother would soak it in water and after squeezing out as much of the water as she could she would then place it in a warm oven. As the bread dried out it gave off a smell of freshly baked bread.

Church of the Most Precious Blood

When it was taken out of the oven it felt warm and fresh. We all tended to gorge ourselves on the warm bread with or without margarine on it. What food we had left over from Sunday was served up on Monday. My mother would fry cabbage and potatoes on the pan and serve it up as Bubble and Squeak. On Tuesday we were usually fed mashed potatoes and sausages and on Wednesday we were given a plate of Irish stew. On Thursday we were sent to my Aunt Kathleen to be fed. My Aunt Kathleen worked in the local Bachelors tinned foods factory. She would often send down bags of dried prunes to our house. They rarely lasted long enough to be served up as desert. They were eaten up just as quickly as they arrived in the door. One time my brother Brendan convinced me to eat a spoonful of cat food out of a tin. He was supposed to eat some after me but then said that he had changed his mind.

One time my mother wanted to get a job in a café in Dorset Street. My father strongly objected by telling my mother that she had enough to do looking after the family. She later managed to get some work from home. A large box of plastic toilet bags would arrive on our doorstep. We all sat around the fire and put a coloured string through each bag and placed them back into the box. This brought in some extra money to the house. Some of the women from our area would go out to work in the evenings as office cleaners. Others worked part time in Bachelors. It seemed that wherever work was to be had they would seek it out.

70

The Fishmonger

These were great women. They worked twenty four hours a day looking after their homes and families and still managed to find the strength and energy to work part time in local industries. It certainly couldn't have been easy for them or their families. They would arrive home exhausted at the end of the day and were still expected to find time to hand up their husband's dinner or tend to one or more of their children. As soon as the older of the children went out to work at fourteen years of age or younger the sooner more money would come into the home. The more children that went out to work the easier life became for some families. Every penny that came into the home was vital to the family's survival.

Chapter 7

The Cabra Baths

During our school holidays most of us spent the daytime hanging around the open-air Cabra Baths or swimming pool as it was sometimes referred to. Water was fed from the nearby Tolka River into the pool. A wall of about three to four feet high with a small gateway at each end surrounded the swimming area. At one end of the enclosure there was a long covered changing area. Beside this area there were two doors next to each other. One housed the water pump and the other was for the use of the caretaker. There were steps leading into the pool from each corner and also at its middle section. Dublin Corporation was responsible for the baths.

When a boy was getting in for a swim the main thing that he had to watch out for was his towel or whatever piece of rag he had for drying himself off with. It was a regular occurrence for such items to disappear. Girls were never allowed into the swimming baths during normal opening times. Some girls did however manage to use them after hours. They were supposed to use the nearby Silverspoon for swimming in. This was a stretch of the Tolka River that ran alongside the baths. There was also a place called the Broken Arches. On one occasion a dead horse was found floating in the baths.

Tolka River

Most of the boys took full advantage of this and treated the bloated horse as a raft. The big boys would run along the side of the pool and jump out onto the dead horse. The caretaker had some of the bigger boys tie a rope around the neck of the horse and gangs of kids helped the caretaker drag the dead animal up into the shallow area where all the small children swam.

Another time one of the bigger boys defecated in the pool. Everyone screamed at the sight of it and abandoned the water. "Quick mister, there's a big thing in the water". The caretaker grabbed a long pole with a net attached to one end and scooped out the offending item. He threw it over the wall and onto the grass for the flies to feast on. As he stood with the pole in his hand looking like a Greek warrior he told the lads that the water was now okay to get back into. Before the words were out of his mouth the pool was once again full of screaming kids.

Sure I suppose he thought that an extra drop of bleach in the water would sort out any major threat from germs. It didn't much matter that it would burn the eyes out of the children. Maybe that's why they were always screaming. On a hot sunny day nothing would keep the lads from the water. We knew this stretch of the Tolka River as the Silverspoon. It was here that you could catch little fish we called pinkeens.

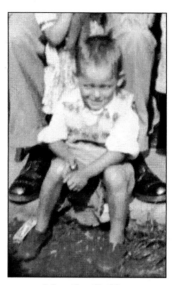

Martin Coffey

There was also an area of swamp along the riverbank where frogs and grasshoppers were found in abundance. The river would overflow in the winter months. Sometimes my mother and her sister Kathleen would bring us and our cousins to the Cardiffbridge end of the Tolka River on the pretence that we were going to the seaside.

Entire families often went to the Cabra baths and sat on the hill overlooking the area while having a picnic. There was never enough hot water at home for washing gangs of young children. The baths was an ideal place to take them to. It was always full of children each day of the school summer holidays. Another area for public outdoor swimming was further up along the Tolka River near Drumcondra, not too far from where the Lemon's sweet factory was once located. There was plenty of changing areas and steps leading down to the river. This stretch of water was capable of accommodating more swimmers than the Cabra baths

The Royal Canal

The nearby Royal Canal also provided a place for children to swim in. Boys could be seen diving and jumping off the humpbacked Broombridge into the canal water below. The canal at this point had a lot of old bicycle frames, prams and dead animals thrown into it.

The Royal Canal Broombridge

It never seemed to bother any of the children that swam there. Amazingly enough it was never known for someone to become sick from swimming in the canal. Maybe there were different types of germs back then. I have often wondered why the canal was never cleaned out on a regular basis regardless of whether it was used for, boating or fishing. The favourite place to swim in the Canal was by the big lock gates near the railway crossing close to Cardiffbridge. The bigger boys would close off one of the lower gates and open the top gate to let the water fill up in between. Although it is only a short distance across from one side to the other I never ventured in. I was unable to swim and wasn't too keen to learn. I never had the courage to jump into the canal water like other boys had. Most of the boys had no swim wear and so jumped or dived into the canal naked. They would then run around or trick act with each other on the canal bank to get themselves dry.

William Rowan Hamilton

There is a plaque erected to William Rowan Hamilton on the wall along the canal footpath almost under Broombridge. Hamilton was a scientist associated with Dunsink Observatory. In 1843 William Hamilton was looking for ways of extending complex numbers to higher spatial dimensions. He eventually tried four dimensions and created quaternion. This mathematical equation was used in modern times by N.A.S.A. to ensure that the Mars Reconnaissance Orbiter achieved its goal in 2006.

W.R. Hamilton Plaque

Throughout the years mathematicians the world over have been known to visit this site at Broombridge. All of this information of course meant nothing to the vast majority of the people of Cabra West. Most of them had a problem adding up two plus two never mind trying to solve scientific mathematics. It is quite probable that very few people from Cabra West new or understood anything of the plaque commemorating William Hamilton. However the people of Cabra West have come to claim Hamilton as one of their own and recently named a small housing complex for senior citizens after him.

The Seaside

The best place of all that my mother brought us to was the beach. A trip to the beach usually brought us to Portmarnock or Dollymount Strand. This entailed two bus trips and must have put some strain on my mother's purse. We would all run across the old wooden bridge and up through the sand dunes onto Dollymount beach. We always brought a couple of bottles of water to drink and an assortment of cheese, boiled egg and tomato sandwiches to eat. At the beach sand would get almost everywhere and especially in the sandwiches. You would feel it grinding between your teeth as you bit down on a soggy tomato sandwich. The tide always appeared to be fully out anytime we were there. We would have to walk out miles before it came up to our knees. Once you got yourself wet you had to run around to dry off, as we would seldom have a towel to share between us all.

76

Dollymount Strand

My mother kept us out all day to ensure that we fell down exhausted when we finally got to our beds. In a couple of photographs of our family at the beach you can see me wearing a large pair of girl's knickers. They probably belonged to one of my big sisters. A trip out on Sunday with both my parents would either bring us by train to Bray or Portmarnock.

One time my father paid for some of us to go out in a rowing boat in Bray. There were no such things as life jackets or safety warnings given. Once you stepped into the boat you were at the mercy of the elements. The further out we went the colder we became. It was all very well standing on the beach with the sun shining down on us as we wore our summer shorts and vests but a few feet out on the water made a big difference. Out there it was freezing.

A large majority of Dublin families took to the beach during the summer. There were ice cream vendors, donkey or horse rides along the beach and of course there was always someone selling boiled water to make your own tea with. We always enjoyed a day out at the beach. It was cheap entertainment. My lasting memory of being at the seaside as a child is that it was always freezing cold. No matter where I stood or tried to hide, a sharp ice wind would always find me. My little spindly legs would shiver and shake like reeds on a riverbank. I was just a skinny little thing that would disappear when turned sideways.

Entrance to Kilmainham Gaol

Irish History

My mother would often take a group of us children on a day out. This could entail a visit to places of historical interest in and around Dublin such as Dublin Castle or Christchurch cathedral. She appeared to know quite a lot of the history of the city and its environs. She instilled into me a great love for Irish history. Another place my mother would often take us into was graveyards. She would walk us for hours around Glasnevin cemetery. She seemed to love reading the information on the headstones. We were very often dragged from Museum to Graveyard to Art Gallery on a fine summer's day. It was a cheap day out with no admission fee being charged.

My mother would bring sandwiches to eat and a bottle of water for us to share amongst each other. She called the sandwiches Dagwood Sandwiches. There were three slices of bread to each sandwich with whatever filling she had put in between. You could end up with a pain in your jaw from overstretching your mouth to try and get a full bite of bread into your gob. From all of the fresh air we had and the walking that we did it never mattered what was placed in front of us to eat. If we were hungry enough we would eat anything. My mother walked us almost everywhere because it was the cheapest form of transport available to us.

St. Catherine's Convent School

Chapter 8

Early Schooldays and Free Milk

Because we had so many young children my mother was entitled to a certain amount of free milk from the government. A house on upper Killala Road was designated as a kind of milk depot. It was run by Mrs Hall. I would go there each morning before school to collect whatever quantity of milk we were entitled to. The crates of milk were stacked up at the side of the house. I would hand in a pink card that had to be initialled or stamped to say that I had been given our quota for that particular day. Brendan made a wooden milk bottle carrier in the tech. I used this to carry the milk home in. My mother gave me one-shilling pocket money every week for collecting the milk each morning.

The Convent

Our entire family of fifteen children all attended Saint Catherine's Convent School. My grandmother did not approve of my two older sisters being sent to the convent. She was reared in one when she was a child and had a great dislike for the nuns. One day my brother Noel who was at this time about seven years old brought my Brother Brendan to school with him. Brendan was only about three years old.

Anne Coffey School Photo

I'm not too sure what age I was when I started attending school. I think I started when I was about four years old. I missed a years schooling because of an accident I had. On my first day in school I remember seeing my mother looking in through the window at me. We were allowed to play with empty cigarette cartons and matchboxes. We used them as building blocks. My first teacher in the convent school was Miss Courtney. I suppose she was probably no more than nineteen or twenty years old at the time. To me however she seemed ancient. That was when I was in Low-Babies. When I graduated into High Babies I was chosen to play in a musical group. We were to perform on stage in front of our mothers. I had to play the triangle. I was envious of a boy named Kevin Caulfield because he got to play the drum. I remember seeing my mother sitting in the front row on a long wooden bench as we played.

First taste of the Strap

When I moved into First Class I had Sister Mary Oliver. I became her pet. She would always choose me to erase the blackboard for her. She also had me selling Lucky Lumps for her during our lunch break. A very odd time a Lucky Lump might have a threepenny piece inside it, hence its name. One time I was sent to the nun's living quarters on a message. I remember seeing a whole clothesline of dark navy coloured knickers hanging up. To me they seemed enormous and much bigger than my older sister's ones.

Catherine Coffey

When I got home I told my brother about them. He said it was a sin to look at nun's knickers. The boys play area was at the front of the school building and the girls' area was situated around the back. A teacher or Nun would patrol the dividing line to ensure that neither sex passed over the forbidden line. No conversation or contact was allowed between the sexes. I could look at my younger sister but I was forbidden to talk to her.

Being very young and innocent was to prove no excuse for being late for school. As you entered the school you immediately headed for the cloakroom to hang up your little coat or jacket. One of the nuns who resembled Charles Bronson would stand at the entrance to the cloakroom. She was tall and had a moustache. She stood there with a grin on her face and held a large brown strap in her hand. A bunch of keys and the strap usually hung like a gunfighter's weapon from a belt tied around her waist.

One morning I was no more than a few minutes late. As I walked out of the cloakroom past the nun I suddenly heard a swishing noise. This was followed by a most excruciating pain across the back of my legs. I went tumbling along the well-polished corridor floor screaming in agony. I had no idea what had happened to me. I looked behind me and saw a large dark figure screaming at me. Because I was slow in getting to my feet the nun came running after me with the strap raised. I scurried along the floor in terror and finally finding my feet ran for my life.

Communion Girls

Early School Life

Each school day we were given a small bottle of milk and a sandwich for our lunch. Except on Wednesday that is, because then we were given a current bun. Each Wednesday I was given an extra bun for helping out. As teacher's pet I had the job of counting how many boys in my class had to get lunch. I would write the figure down on a piece of slate board along with our class number. I would then go directly to the kitchen area where a deaf and dumb woman worked. I would show her the figures on the slate and return to my classroom.

After a while the woman from the kitchen would arrive outside our room with the correct amount of milk and sandwiches. I would answer her knock on the door and hold it open. In an orderly manner each little boy took a sandwich and bottle of milk with him outside to the play area or schoolyard. Every Friday we were given jam sandwiches. Absolutely nothing went to waste as milk and sandwiches quickly disappeared into hungry little mouths. Once we entered the school building we were strictly forbidden to talk. As a child who came from a family of talkers I found this quite difficult to keep to.

Black Babies

The silver tops off the milk bottles had to be saved for the Little Black Babies who were starving in Africa. Well that is what we were told. Every child was expected to donate one penny to these Black Babies. We also had to bring in any silver paper that we could find at home.

Anne Coffey First Holy Communion

One of my older brothers was working at this time and he would bring home empty tea chests to our house, usually on Friday. We would kill each other as children trying to tear out the sliver paper that lined the inside of the tea chests. The Nun's sold the silver paper on to a recycling depot somewhere and supposedly used the money they got for the Black Babies. They never gave any of this money to the Little White Babies of Cabra West who were just as hungry as any children found on the African Continent. We were inundated in school with stories of Africa and how poor the people were. With all of the lands and money that the Church had why couldn't they pay for the food instead of taking it out of the mouths of the poor people of Cabra West? After all we had neighbours who were very poor with plenty of little mouths to be fed.

Christmas Treat

On our last day before Christmas Sister Mary Oliver would have an assortment of Christmas items displayed on her desk. She would call out each little boy in order and let him choose which gift he wanted. There was a little Cardboard Crib, a Plastic Snow Ornament that you could shake and make it snow inside, a statue of Our Lady that would shine in the dark and many other things besides. I always chose the shining statue. I would hide under the bed covers with it and watch it glow. I thought it was magic. I loved the Convent.

Tony Coffey and Brian Burke

First Holy Communion

Like many other boys of my age I had to make my First Holy Communion before leaving the convent school. I remember standing around the classroom wall and the Parish Priest coming in and asking us a question each. We had to memorize certain questions and answers from our little green covered Catechism book. "Who made the world...God made the world. Who is God...God is our father in Heaven, the creator and Lord of all things."

We certainly had no understanding of what we were saying. We just rattled it off as best we could and hoped that it was correct. It was like most lessons in school. We learned them off by heart and just recited them back to the teacher. There was certainly no attempt to help us understand what we were saying. There are some things we never forget.

The Priest and Nuns gave us stern warnings about the evils of Protestant Churches. We were taught to place one hand by the side of our face when passing by a Protestant Church to avoid the temptation to look inside the door. Didn't we know that the Devil himself was lurking inside that door, waiting to grab a hold of any poor unsuspecting little Holy Catholic child passing by?

Convent Grotto

It left me curious about the little red coloured Protestant Church in Phibsborough that sheltered in the shadow of the nearby very imposing Catholic Church of Saint Peter. One time my mother brought us walking into town and took us in to see Christchurch Cathedral. I refused to go in because it was Protestant. A sharp clip to the ear told me in no uncertain terms that my mother's law over-ruled any Canon Law then in existence. When it came time to practise receiving Holy Communion the Nun would have us stick out our tongue. She would place a small piece of ice-cream wafer on it. We had to keep our tongue out until she gave the word.

We were warned that the wafer was not to touch our teeth and most of all that we were not to drop it onto the ground. That was considered a sin. We were to swallow the wafer without chewing on it. This was quite a difficult task because the wafer immediately stuck to the roof of your mouth. Under no circumstances were we allowed to touch the wafer with our hands. These were the sacred rules of receiving Holy Communion.

We also had to prepare for our first confession so that we could be found in a state of grace. We had to be cleansed of all sins. What sins little innocent children could possibly be guilty of I could never understand. Most times we went to confession we had to make up sins to tell the priest. We certainly had no idea what we were doing or why we were doing it. I have little or no recollection of the actual day of my First Holy Communion. I do know that it took place in the chapel within the grounds of the Convent School.

Convent cloakroom

Both my parents and possibly my Granny Burke would have been present. The adults may have been given a cup of tea and a sandwich afterwards. I remember having my photograph taken beside a little grotto or group of statues near to the chapel. That photograph mysteriously disappeared in later years. My father would have done the usual rounds of his relations with me. I would have been given money from each of the adults that we met. This money was supposedly to offset the cost that my parents had incurred when dressing me for the occasion. I knew nothing of this of course. Money was always something that adults always seemed to have plenty of when it was needed. I had no idea what my parents had to go through to get it. Up to recent times I still had my little First Holy Communion certificate. On the reverse side I wrote a promise that I would say my prayers every night.

One day a strange man arrived in our classroom. The nun told us to take our schoolbags and follow the man. Nobody ever told us that this was our graduation day into the big boy's school, Saint Finbarr's. We had no idea who this strange man was. Anyway we said our goodbyes to Sister Mary Oliver and the convent school and headed off into the sunset. As we marched two by two in a little line behind our new schoolmaster Mister Byrne, he lit up his pipe and hummed a tune all the way to our new school. It wasn't really a new school of course because it was originally built in 1943. My father often referred to it as the redbrick College. We were led like little lambs along the roadway to our new institute of education, the big school.

Old School Desk

I would come to love my new teacher just as much as I had loved Sister Mary Oliver. She died sometime in 1980 and I believe that she was buried in her hometown down the country. The original attendance roll for the convent states that I started school on the 1st of July 1957 and Finbarr's school records show that I attended there from 1960 until 1965. By all accounts it would appear that I was a relatively bright young lad in both schools.

Looking back it seems to me that both sets of teachers that I had took a good approach to teaching, they made it interesting and rewarding. I suppose other children were not so fortunate. So many of the children came from families that struggled more so than my own. A lot of them were unwashed from one week to the next and always looked as though they were on the brink of starvation. There were a few boys that came to school covered in bruises from beatings that their father or mother had given them. Did anyone ever tell the black babies in Africa about that?

St. Finbarr's School

Chapter 9

The Big School

The new school was quite different from the school we had come from. It was not quite so clean and quiet and certainly not as orderly as the Convent was. On my first day in Finbarr's there seemed to be hundreds of boys running around the schoolyard screaming and shouting. There were milk crates rattling and boys throwing bread at each other. We had about thirty-six children or so in the new class. I knew most of them from my class in the convent but there were some faces that were new to me. I was seated in the row of desks nearest to the classroom door.

On a ledge above the blackboard there were three little chalk figures or busts. One was Pope John XXIII, one was Patrick Pearse and the other was of James Connolly. We were to be taught a lot about these three individuals and the roles they played in the fight for Irish freedom. Pride of place was given to a small tricolour flag. My teacher was very aware that some of his pupils were almost illiterate. He later set up a special class to help them along.

My New Teacher

My new teacher was Mister Byrne a great lover of the Irish language and also traditional Irish music. He took great delight in showing us boys how to perform a hornpipe or jig.

My teacher Paddy Bán

As we queued up outside the toilets he would tap out a dance on the red tiled floor. He was also a great flute player. He would bring his beautiful instrument into the class and gently take it out of the black box in which it was encased. We would all sit and listen entranced by the music that filled our classroom. This was an experience that I had never before been exposed to. Once a week we were taught lessons on the tin whistle. To me these music periods were heaven.

Each Monday morning our teacher would arrive in the classroom with pieces of blood soaked toilet paper stuck to his face. The poor man would have a throbbing hangover from the night before. His face was cut to pieces by the blunt razor he had shaved with that morning. We were quietly ordered to place our folded arms on our desks and to rest our heads on them. Monday was always a quiet and slow day. Each morning our teacher would cycle from his home on Blackhorse Avenue to the school. Each morning at ten o'clock I would hurry down the corridor to the teacher's room. One cup of hot sweet tea was quickly handed to me and I would bring it to my teacher. Once he had his tea he would perk up a little. Other boys would often spit into their teacher's tea or stir it with their fingers. We all remember the swishing sound of the teacher's little bamboo cane as it landed with a sting on our outstretched hand. No one escaped being punished, some boys more so than others.

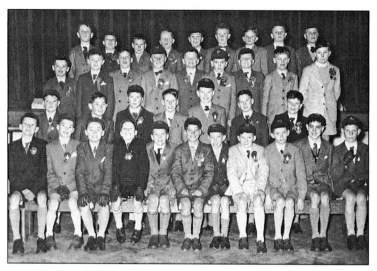

Finbarr's School Confirmation Group about 1959

It was a frightening sight to see our teacher out of control as he would throw a boy across his desk and beat him almost senseless.

The Cane

When the teacher was finished the boy would lie on the classroom floor doubled up in pain. The teacher would stand trembling with spit dripping from his mouth. He would run his hand through his hair and proceed to warn the rest of us to never step out of line. It almost seemed as if my teacher had a duel personality, one that was full of music and dance and the other full of anger and rage. I suppose we all have our faults and failings but there were times when I felt that our teacher had gone a little bit too. Another teacher who later became the principle would make boys in his class bend over their desk with their little trousers dropped down around their ankles. He would absolutely leather them senseless. There were good schooldays and bad schooldays.

My teacher often told me that I looked like Saint Dominic Savio. There was a picture of him hanging on the wall in the hallway right outside our classroom door. He was a boy-saint who died at the age of fifteen and was canonized in 1954. One time my friend Willie and I were late for school. We had to try and sneak past the open door of the headmaster's classroom. Try as we may we were caught.

Martin Coffey

He brought us into his office and accused us of trying to steal a lock and chain off the school gates. He swore blind that he had seen us. I don't know what he saw but it certainly wasn't what he claimed. I denied it totally and received three of the best on each hand. My friend was a little smarter than me. He more or less said yes that we were guilty as charged. He was sent on to our classroom. I was beaten to within an inch of my life. From my fingertips to the crook of my arm he lashed me with his cane. The skin on my hands split open and bled. I refused to cry. My arms were covered in welts and bruises. When he eventually sent me to my class I was almost passing out with the pain I felt.

My teacher was shocked at the state of my arms and sent me to the toilets to soak them in cold water. This is probably the only time I was beaten in the wrong at school. I have seen the results of beatings other boys were given by different teachers and some of the beatings were brutal in the extreme. Sometime later the same headmaster tried to do exactly the same thing with another boy. The boy broke from the teacher's grasp and made for the office door. The teacher ran after him but fell to the floor dead. He died of a heart attack. I think a newspaper accused the boy of killing the teacher. Up to this point I always thought this man was a great teacher. He gave me and other boys a job in Croke Park every Sunday selling programmes.

Anne Coffey

Confirmation Day

I made my confirmation from Finbarr's School. Each day leading up to the occasion we were frog marched over to the church. If I stood at the top of the steps at the front of the church and looked up at the spire I would faint and fall to the ground. One of my pals would have to bring me home. We used this ploy on more than one occasion. John Charles McQuaid confirmed the bunch of us. My older brothers had warned me that the priest would give me a hard slap in the face. They told me that I was not to cry even though it was going to be a really hard slap that I would get. I had to be strong to become a soldier of Christ. I was terrified as I approached this solemn looking man in red. One of my friends from Fassaugh Avenue had said he would hit him back and run out of the church. Much to my mother's horror I spent most of my Confirmation money on art materials that I had bought in Woolworth's.

Mitching

When any boys were missing from our class during roll call at ten o'clock I was usually sent to get a note from their mother's. We called this mitching. Almost every boy that went mitching from school would hide his schoolbag under a garden hedge near the school. At that time not too many mother's in Cabra West could read or write. A missing boy would often meet me on my journey to his house and ask me to write a note from his mother to the teacher.

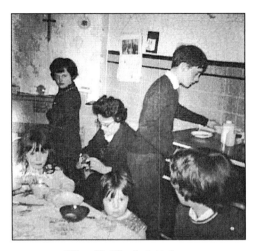

The Coffey's kitchen

This is how I was never short of sweets or comics. They paid up or else. I mitched once from the Tech and was bored waiting for my friends to finish school for the day.

Priests and Confession

One time my friends and I were sitting as quietly as we could outside the confession box of the parish priest. We were swapping what sins we were going to tell him. The next thing we knew was that the priest let out a roar and we all leapt into the air. The priest came charging like a bull out of the confessional with his bulging red face framed in his black cassock. He grabbed open the door where a young boy was and dragged him out by the scruff of the neck. He kept roaring and calling the boy a little liar. As he dragged the screaming boy out towards the main door of the church my friends and I almost trampled on each other as we made a break for the side exit.

It turned out that the boy had confessed to the priest about stealing fruit from outside a shop on the Cabra Road. He told the priest he had done so because he was starving and that his mother had no money to buy food to feed the family with. I have never forgotten this experience and always wondered why the priest never investigated the boy's story to see if the Church could help.

Tony & June Coffey

As a young boy I was told to always address a priest with the words "God bless you father". One day I was walking near my home in a twilight zone of childish thought. I never saw the priest coming towards me but I certainly felt the back of his hand as he lashed out and slapped me across the face. I ended up sprawled on the ground looking dazed with a "What did I do" expression on my face. The priest scowled and called me "a little get". I never made that mistake again.

The Priest and the Brush

One local man told me that as a young boy he had polio and was unable to attend school. His mother had him seated in the front garden in the sunshine while she carried on with her housework. The Parish Priest came along and seeing the young boy asked him why he was not in school. The boy explained as best he could that the nun's had refused to take him into the convent school on account of him having polio. The Parish Priest became furious at this accusation and lashed out at the young boy with a walking stick. The force of the blow sent the boy sprawling across the garden. The noise of the commotion brought the boy's mother to the door but the Priest had gone. As she picked the boy up from the ground he told his mother what had happened. The boy's mother tied on her headscarf as she grabbed for her sweeping brush.

The two Bernards

She ran towards the shops after the Priest. She caught up with him as he was talking to a group of women. She laid into him with the brush and gave him a stern warning to keep clear of her son. No doubt the onlookers had great stories of that event to tell for years to come. Some years later this priest died and was buried beside the grotto in the church grounds.

One time a Priest came to our house around Easter time. He came to collect his Easter Dues. He would sit at our kitchen table talking to my father. My mother was always ignored. He would ask my father about the family in England, my brother's and sister. "Are they attending Mass every Sunday Mister Coffey" he would ask. My father would lie through his teeth as he said "Yes Father and Holy Communion too".

 I somehow knew that my brother's were certainly not attending any church in England. I was about to say something to the Priest about it when my father gave me a look that only father's could give. I kept my mouth firmly shut. I was warned afterwards to say absolutely nothing when the Priest came to our house. Why did the priest ask my father for money? We barely had enough to feed ourselves without having to feed him too.

Mary Coffey with Joseph and Helen

School Concerts

For a while I played on the hurling team for my school. We mostly played in the Phoenix Park. One time we needed new jerseys and hurleys so our teacher organised a concert. I remember sitting in the school hall with some of my brothers as Dickie Rock jumped around on the stage singing. Ronnie Drew and the Dubliners also played to us that night. There were several other acts of which I have no recollection but they were all there to support a good cause. I remember it as a great night's entertainment. Over the years there was always some kind of concert being performed in the school hall. There was some great musical and acting talent in Cabra West. I also remember when the stage curtain was purposely set on fire one weekend while the school was closed.

We often played football in the schoolyard. Another game we played was Pussy Four Corners. It was mainly the younger boys that played this game. A person stood in each corner and another stood in the middle. The idea was to exchange places with another boy before the boy in the middle beat you to that corner. If you lost then you had to stand in the middle. Chasing each other around the yard was probably the most popular thing we did. Anything was better than being locked up in our classroom all day long.

Lord Gough 1957

Lord Gough

In 1957 a statue was blown up in the Phoenix Park. It was that of Field Marshal Lord Gough. The I.R.A. caused the explosion. Supposedly the remains of the statue were sold to Chillingham Castle in Northumberland England. The statue was restored and re erected there in 1990. It was originally unveiled in the Phoenix Park on the 21st February 1880. In 1944 the head was taken off the statue and thrown into the river Liffey and in 1956 the horse's leg was blown off. On the day of the explosion in 1957 quite a large crowd of Dubliners gathered in the Phoenix Park as Dublin Corporation arranged for the disposal of the broken horse and rider.

Because Cabra West is so close to the Phoenix Park any major event that took place there became local knowledge within a short space of time. The majority of people from Cabra West couldn't care less whether the statue remained or was removed from the park. Either way it didn't put any extra food on the table or money in their purse. These people had more important things to worry about than some old statue being blown up. Like Nelson's Pillar I suppose it was almost inevitable that it would go up with a bang at some point in time. Lord Gough had served under the Duke of Wellington in the Peninsular Wars. He was severely wounded in battle and that is why the statue of his horse was displayed with one leg raised. Two legs raised meant that the rider was killed in battle.

Liam Whelan's grave

Liam Whelan

On the 6th February of the following year 1958 Liam Whelan from Cabra was killed in what became known as the Munich Air Disaster. Liam and several other members of the Manchester United football team had perished in the plane crash. A British European Airways flight crashed in a snow blizzard on its third attempt at take-off. The plane was carrying the full Manchester United football team, backroom staff, journalists and supporters. There were forty-three passengers on board and twenty-three of these lost their lives. Manchester United had just beaten Red Star Belgrade in the European Cup. The plane had landed in Munich airport to refuel. Liam Whelan was a great inspiration to many young budding football stars from Cabra West. He made ninety-eight first-team appearances between 1955 and 1958.

Liam is buried on the railway side of Glasnevin cemetery. On a bright sunlit winters morning at eleven thirty on the 8th of December 2006 a plaque was finally unveiled to Liam Whelan and a bridge in Cabra named in his honour. A great crowd turned out for this historic occasion. The Lord Mayor of Dublin Vincent Jackson carried out the unveiling of the plaque and the naming of the bridge. Another great football legend and survivor of the air disaster was in attendance. Sir Bobby Charlton arrived amid a great throng of people that were there to support the occasion.

Nelson's Pillar 1966

Nelson's Pillar

In the very early hours of a March morning in 1966 a large explosion was heard right across Dublin city and its suburbs. Looking at their clocks and watches through sleepy eyes Dubliners noted the time as 2am. Some people on the Northside of the city reckoned it was a jailbreak from Mountjoy Prison. Others believed it to be a ship exploding on the quayside. The noise shook houses and homes as far away as Cabra West, two miles to the north of the city centre. Nobody it seemed ever imagined that the real cause of the noise was the demise of Nelson's Pillar in the heart of Dublin's O'Connell Street.

The explosion ripped apart the upper half of the pillar and spewed the shattered remains of Admiral Nelson's statue across the street below. Very little damage however was caused to nearby shops and premises. One taxi driver passing the pillar at the moment of the explosion escaped unhurt. A Cabra woman actually saw the explosion as it happened. She was standing at the window of the nearby Metropole ballroom at the time. She could never publicly say anything about it because if her father had known where she was she would have found herself in very hot soup.

Doyle's Corner Phibsborough

Some people were surprised that Nelson had lasted so long. For others it was a constant reminder of all that the British Empire represented. It stood at 121 feet high and was made of granite. It was erected in 1808 under the instructions of the then Lord Lieutenant of Ireland. The Pillar was used as the main tram terminus for Dublin.

The entrance money into the Pillar was donated to charity. In 1960 An Taoiseach Séan Lemass had suggested that the Pillar should be removed from the main thoroughfare of the city. It was always a great meeting point for people regardless of what part of the country they came to Dublin from. It was often said that no true Dubliner ever went up to the top of the Pillar.

As the news of the explosion was broadcast over the State Radio people throughout the Republic were astounded. The Pillar was always viewed as a central meeting point for visitors to the city. Nelson's Pillar had stood on this spot for the best part of 148 years. Two days after the explosion Irish Army Engineers blew up the remaining stump along with nearly every shop window in O'Connell Street. They caused more damage than the IRA. Many people collected pieces of the remaining rubble as souvenirs. My brother Noel has a piece. Another connection that Noel has with the Pillar is the time himself and Thomas Crawley peed off the top of it onto the flower seller below. They were only young lads and by the time they had climbed up all of the steps and reached the top they were bursting for a pee.

June, Catherine, Helen, Tony & Joe Coffey

One vivid memory that has stayed with me from my childhood was that of a funeral procession in 1960. Our entire school of boys were marched in an orderly and sombre fashion along Fassaugh Avenue and down towards Phibsborough. In fact all of the schools in the area marched their pupils in a likewise fashion to the same destination. We were lined up along the roadway opposite the Bohemian Cinema. At that time there was a row of cottages with long front gardens where Phibsborough Shopping Centre is today. Some of us sat or stood on the walls of the cottages.

I didn't really understand why we were there so I asked my teacher. He told me and a few other boys that Irish soldiers had been killed by black men. The only black men we knew of were in the films with Tarzan. A funeral cortège approached from Doyle's Corner. I remember seeing a lot of soldiers marching along with the cortège. When the funeral had passed by we were all allowed to go home early from school.

I didn't understand what it was all about. I had no idea where the Congo was until our teacher showed us on a map the following day. What were Irish soldiers doing in Africa anyway some of us had asked. Nothing seemed to make sense to me back then. I was to later learn that on the 28th of July in 1960, Baluba tribesmen massacred eight Irish soldiers. Lieutenant Colonel Murt Buckley led the men of the 32nd Irish Battalion on a peacekeeping mission to the Congo. The ambush took place at Niemba as the Irish soldiers tried to repair a bridge over the Luweyeye River

Belvedere Football Team

Sunday Football

There was always a football game going on somewhere in the neighbourhood. Most every road had its own team that would compete against other roads. I remember Mister Bennett from Rathoath Road being very involved in football teams. In later years it became more serious as a tarmac soccer pitch was made in the grounds of the church. Every evening crowds would gather to cheer on their own particular road. These were great events. More less serious football games were played on the road where you lived. You could always get a better bounce on the ball when you played on the road. Most of my friends hated playing football in the field on our road. There were too many holes for a start and the ground was too rough and bumpy to run on.

Some Sunday mornings a football game would commence right near to our house. All the bigger lads would play against each other. One morning as the game was in progress a police squad car drove down the road. All the players would scatter in several directions like a well-rehearsed ballet. Because of the layout of the area it was easy to make an escape by running along the side entrance of some corner houses and break through to the next road. Because there were so many lads scattering in so many different directions it made it next to impossible for the Gardai to catch anyone. As one of the lads made good his escape he kicked the ball away before running off.

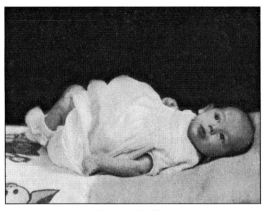
Tony Coffey

Within seconds the road was cleared of all those lads that had taken part in the game. A young couple were walking down the road as all of this action was taking place. They were more interested in each other than anything that was happening around them. The ball stopped near to where they were passing by. The young man kicked the ball back in the direction from where it had come from. The squad car pulled up alongside the young couple and the young man was arrested for playing football. He had a hearing difficulty and was unaware of what was happening.

Within seconds his family that lived nearby were informed. His father and several brothers along with some of their neighbours marched on the local police station. After some time they arrived back at their house accompanied by several squad cars. A very large crowd had gathered outside their house. The police ordered the crowd to move on. Someone from the crowd shouted back that they are the ones that should move on. The police baton-charged the crowd and all hell broke loose. My older brother Bernard shouted at me to run home as the attack turned nasty.

Gambling schools and football playing in the streets was strictly frowned upon by the Gardai. On the odd occasion a Garda would arrive on our road on his bicycle. If he saw myself and my friends having a game of cards he would take the deck of cards from us and warn us not to be gambling. We only played for matchsticks or buttons.

Anne, Catherine and Martin Coffey

Sometimes on a Sunday night as we lay in bed a row would break out between a husband and wife. We had a grandstand view of the action from our bedroom window. Punches and spitting would go to and fro between the couple and maybe a knife would suddenly appear in the woman's hand. Michael Barry would most always be the neighbour to break up the fighting. He was the John Wayne of the neighbourhood. In general there was never any trouble amongst our neighbours.

It was often reckoned that if an adult corrected a child then the child must have been up to no good and an odd time one of them might give you a clip on the ear for getting up to mischief. If you mentioned this to your parents you could come out much worse. It was the same if I came home from school and told of the teacher giving me six of the best for doing nothing. I was sent straight up to bed for the rest of the day.

There was no worse punishment for young children than to have them cooped up in a bedroom with nothing to keep them amused. This especially applied to me as all I wanted was to be outside playing with my friends. I can think of nothing worse than looking out of my bedroom window watching my friends playing cowboys and Indians or not being in a position to help in the shoot out at the O.K. Corral.

Religious Pageant

Chapter 10

Religious Observance

Religion played a great part in the lives of the people of Cabra West. Every Sunday the local church was packed to capacity with worshippers. Sometimes late comers would have to stand outside the church door. There was always a group of men who could be seen kneeling on one knee at the back of the church. One priest referred to these as 'duck hunters'. Ten o'clock mass was the children's mass. Sometimes if you were lucky you could get to go up onto the balcony and sit in the front row. Here you had a great view of all the bald headed old fellas below. Sometimes my friends and I would play a game at counting all the bald heads.

The sound of the organ could be heard outside as you approached the steps of the church. That sound meant you were late for Mass. Mister Mack the blind man played the organ. He knew all of the hymns off by heart. He also had a little kiosk type shop at the beginning of Carnlough Road. Some lads would try to slip him a fake coin or an old washer and he would chuck it back in their face. He seemed to know every trick in the book and was never caught out by the smart lads. Every year there was the May Procession and the Corpus Christi (Body of Christ) Procession. The May procession was usually lead by two members of the local scout group holding a flag each.

May Procession

These were followed by young girls dressed in white dresses and wearing white veils. They would have their hands held in prayer or could possibly hold their little white Holy Communion book in their hands. The girls followed a platform held up by four scouts. On the platform was a statue of Holy Mary surrounded by a white veil and flowers. There was also white ribbons' reaching from her crown to the platform. As the procession marched through the streets people would sing hymns of praise to Mary. "Hail Holy Queen, mother of mercy." Each year the Parish Priest would select a road to lead the procession. Some houses would have a little alter set up in their front garden or at their front door, especially if the procession was passing them by.

Most every house had buntings tied from the upstairs window to their railings below. For the few days leading up to the procession neighbours could be seen whitewashing all the footpaths along the proposed route. Eventually the procession would be brought to a halt at a chosen location for a mass to be said by the Parish Priest. One time it was in our field. A big wooden alter was erected the night before and all the men gave a hand to put it up. It was a very serious and solemn business. Everyone was keen to help out. Women would arrange bunches of flowers on the alter and have ribbons streaming over it.

Hanging Buntings

The Corpus Christi procession was similar to the May procession. The only major difference was that the procession was led by a group of men from the parish and behind them was the parish priest. Some of the men of the parish or maybe a group of scouts would carry a canopy that was held over the head of the priest. The priest walked through the streets holding aloft a piece of Holy Communion encased in a golden sunburst monstrance. People from the neighbourhood would follow behind the priest carrying holy banners. An open air Mass was once held in the nearby convent grounds with an alter placed high up on a balcony. Another time the Mass was held outside the main entrance to Saint Finbarr's school.

Sodality

Another religious occasion was the Sodality. I have little or no recollection of what type of format they took. I remember seeing a priest cycling down our road one Friday evening and shouting at my older brother to get to Sodality. He dragged myself and Brendan with him to the church. Each road in the area was represented in the church by a card placed on a pole showing the name of your road. That is where you had to sit. You were not allowed to sit anywhere else only in the row allocated to your road.

May Procession

The priest knew every single boy so you could never fool him into thinking you lived on another road. The Priest would stand up in the pulpit and give some kind of sermon. I remember we had to make sure to attend ten o'clock mass the following Sunday. One time when it was close to Communion time and the Parish Priest had his back turned a few of us tried to sneak out of the church. He must have been like my mother with eyes in the back of his head. All of a sudden he let out a roar and screamed at us to get back into our seats. I never liked Sodality because I didn't understand what it was all about.

Why did they never explain it to us in school? I was never too keen on mysterious of religion either. We had to fast from confession on Saturday until Holy Communion on Sunday. Children had to sit at the front of the church. There was always the chance of seeing God inside the little place where the priest got the Communion from. Our teacher told us that once. It was a ploy of course so that the priest could keep an eye on us.

I think that there may have been separate Sodalities for men and women. There were also retreats for the adults. I don't know for sure that there was any for children. My father fell asleep at a retreat one time. He was sitting directly below the pulpit where the priest was bellowing out his sermon from. As my father dozed off he snored out loud.

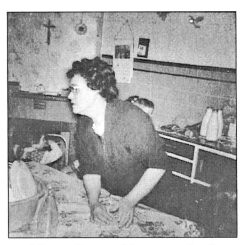
My mother making pancakes?

It probably echoed all around the church because the priest certainly heard it and let out a roar at my poor father. It was well and fine for the priest because he didn't have a house full of fifteen children to provide for. My father worked hard and was always tired out on Friday night. He deserved to rest his eyes.

Easter Sunday/Pancake Tuesday

There was always a great turnout for mass on Easter Sunday and Christmas Day. Every Easter we would tell loads of lies to other children on our road. We would always claim that we got at least eight chocolate Easter Eggs. All of the children would try to outdo each other as to the amount of chocolate eggs they had received. We really only got one large egg and two or three little chocolate-covered marshmallow eggs each. My younger sisters liked to save the coloured silver paper for the nuns. We also got a boiled egg each for our breakfast on Easter morning. My father would draw a face on the eggs for us. He would also put our individual names on the eggs. We loved looking into the big pot of boiling water to see if we could spot which egg we were getting. We always went to ten o' clock Mass on Easter morning.

On Pancake Tuesday we told loads more lies of course about the amount of pancakes we had for our tea. My poor mother would spend hours preparing the pancake batter in preparation for the big feed up at tea time.

Kathleen & Ned Burke

A bag of sugar and several lemons were placed near the cooker as she began the process of churning out as many pancakes in as short a time as she possibly could. There was never enough because no matter how many you were given you still wanted more. My mother would almost collapse from sheer exhaustion and heat as we gorged our little faces around the table. On Ash Wednesday we had a black spot put on our foreheads by the Priest. Some people would still have it there several days later. They must never have washed themselves.

For a young boy a half hour at Mass seemed like an eternity. No sooner had you sat down in your seat when you would have to stand up. No sooner had you stood up when you had to sit down again. Each time the alter boy rang out his little bell you had to bend your head. And so on it went until the men started off coughing. I sometimes wondered who gave them the signal to start. Was it the man hanging on the cross winking down at them? Then the shuffling of feet started as people began heading up to the alter for the Holy Communion. You had to kneel down with your two hands clasped together and your tongue hanging out.

With the communion wafer on your tongue you had to make a reply to the priest as he said "Corpus Christi". "Awhennn" is the nearest audible sound to be given. Whatever you do never let the Holy Communion touch your teeth. To do so was a mortal sin or a mortaler as we called it.

110

Child laid out

The Dead

Everyone in the neighbourhood would turn out for a funeral. The close neighbours of the deceased would all close their curtains on the day. Some people said that if you heard a dog howling it was a sign that someone on your road was going to die. A wake was nearly always held for someone that had died. They were kept at home and laid out for three days. The neighbours came from far and near to pay their respects. Sometimes a particular woman might be sent for to wash the corpse. She might arrive with her daughter who was brought along to learn the trade. Her daughter would set out four candles around the bed and lay out the habit. Sometimes she might help with washing the corpse.

My father told me once that a friend of his had worked in the City Morgue in Amiens Street. A nosey woman from the area would come into the morgue every Friday to have a look at who was laid out. One day she came in and lifted the cover from what she assumed was a corpse. It was my father's friend with a few drinks on him playing a trick. As the poor woman gawked down at him he opened one eye and looked at her. "Hello Maggie" he said. She never came back again, well not alive anyway.

The Confession Box

Kiss the Corpse

If you wanted to avoid being haunted by the deceased you had to touch them or kiss them as they were laid out. One time myself and a few other boys and girls, maybe six or seven of us from our road were sitting on the roundabout wall opposite to a house where a man was laid out dead. During the summer this man would sit in an armchair in his front garden wearing a big woollen overcoat. The garden was all-overgrown with weeds and stingers. To us young children he seemed very strange. His children were never allowed out of the house to play with us. They were always very pale and white skinned. An older boy approached us and said that if we didn't go into the house and kiss the corpse that the dead man would come back and haunt us. The front door of the house was open and almost appeared to beckon us inside.

We had never been inside this house before and it already looked haunted. As we crept up the stairs we held onto each other out of fear. "Oh Mammy" was constantly muttered by each of us as we crept up each step. It was all dark and quiet as we neared the top of the stairs. A faint glow of light emanated from the front bedroom where the corpse lay. Inside the bedroom the tall man was laid out on the bed wearing a brown habit. His arms were crossed over his chest and his face was pasty pale in the glow of four lighted candles that surrounded the bed. Somehow or other I had been pushed to the top of the queue.

Memorial in Cabra West

I nervously peeped around the bedroom door at the corpse laid out on the bed. Suddenly out of nowhere a girl let out an unmerciful scream at the sight of the corpse. As pandemonium broke out the boy standing behind me gave me a shove as he turned to dart for the stairs. I went flying forward and fell face down on the corpse. He was freezing cold but I somehow felt a familiar warm sensation on my legs. I had peed in my trousers with fright. The rest of the boys and girls had stampeded down the stairs like a herd of buffalo in a cowboy film and out to the open field across the road. I came out last and ran straight home to change my wet trousers. I never actually kissed the corpse but came quite close to it. The big boy was right about one thing. The dead man haunted me for months afterwards in my dreams. Anytime my friends and I had to pass that particular house we would always charge past it and let out a scream in terror as if the corpse was coming after us.

Buried Babies

One time a neighbour of ours had little twin babies that had died. My father was approached by their father and asked to make two little coffins to bury the children in. My father put together two very rough boxes made from scraps of wood that he had stored in our back yard. My mother told me of her memory of watching both men walking up the road early one Saturday morning each carrying a little coffin in their arms. Their mother stood at her door crying out like a Banshee at the loss of her two little girls.

113

Belvedere Campout

Like my parents, other neighbours were probably there to give whatever support they could to the grieving couple. The men handed the two little coffins into the man at the main gate of Glasnevin Cemetery for burial. The children's father was not allowed inside the gate to bury his own dead little babies. He probably couldn't afford the time on account of having to go to work. There were other fathers queuing up with their little deceased babies wrapped up in white sheets placed very carefully across the handlebars of their bicycles or held loosely in their arms. Some of the father's would have little homemade coffins carefully balanced on their bicycles or like my father and his neighbour, held safely in their arms A mother never had the opportunity to bury her child or children. Parents never new for sure where their little infants were buried.

My mother once told me that this was a regular occurrence then. She said that children were buried in a mass grave called the Angel's Plot. There was many a baby who was born and died in Cabra West that never went on any official record. When I was brought home from the maternity hospital my mother placed another baby in the bed beside me. A young single girl in our area had given birth to a baby girl without the knowledge of her family. She did however confide in my parents and they offered to help her out in whatever way they could. My mother may have delivered the little infant. The baby girl was born around the same time as I was. My parents had most probably offered to raise the child as their own.

Martin & Brendan Coffey 1968

Would she possibly have been passed off as my twin? My mother probably fed us both from the same breast. The poor little creature however was weak and sickly. She only managed to live for a few weeks before dying. She too was probably wrapped up in a little white sheet and delivered to the gateman in Glasnevin. There was no doctor in attendance to explain why the baby died. It was generally accepted that if a child was poorly and died then it was God's will. No one else in our neighbourhood had any knowledge of this little baby girl being born or dying. She probably went to the Angel's Plot too.

Christmas at Home

I remember one Christmas Eve standing up in the kitchen sink while one of my older sisters washed me. I would then step out onto a chair and be dried off by a second sister. We never wore pyjamas back then. Each one of us little ones would sit around the blazing fire and gaze up at the Christmas tree standing in the corner of the kitchen. Decorations would hang from the ceiling and the walls were filled with Christmas cards. My father always considered himself a handyman on anything electrical. However he always found the Christmas lights a greater challenge. He would curse under his breath as he fiddled with blown bulbs, broken bulbs and bulbs that just refused to work.

Coffey Christmas

His persistence always seemed to pay off and he'd stick his chest out with pride as each one eventually gave in to his demands and lit up. Well, for the moment anyway. Our house was always spotlessly cleaned for Christmas. The skirting boards along the bottom of the walls were dusted and washed as well as all of the doors. The windows were cleaned using newspaper and paraffin oil or water. Even the brass doorknocker and letterbox were polished.

My father would spend hours writing out Christmas cards to send to family and friends across the world. He would have a list made out of people to send them to. Every now and then he would stop and talk to my mother about the person whose card he was writing. They would go off on a tandem of thought that would eventually lead back to the card in hand. My parent's knew so many people and had so many friends.

It was always so hard to sleep with the anticipation and excitement at the thought of Santa Clause. We would try to stay awake until our parents went to bed. Just as I was sinking into a world of dreams something would occur to disturb them. Suddenly my dreams became invaded by whispering voices followed by the scuffle of tiny little feet scurrying across our bedroom floor. The older children would warn us not to make any noise as we crept like little mice down the stairs.

The Coffey's at the seaside 1955

The Christmas lights would illuminate the kitchen in a rainbow of magical colours like a fairyland dream. Our eyes would almost pop out of our little heads as we caught a glimpse of the presents neatly laid out at the foot of the Christmas tree. Our names were neatly written on little pieces of paper to indicate who got what. Wrapping paper was torn apart and little stockings dived into as each child eagerly opened their presents. Everyone was keen to see what Santa Clause had brought them. We would charge up the stairs to waken up our father and mother and maybe the older members of the family who were still asleep. An odd one or two would climb back into bed clutching some of their new toys. I'd fall asleep wearing my little cowboy suit. One time my sister Anne got a Cowgirl outfit. It was turquoise in colour and had a little frilled skirt and hat. The two of us looked like twins standing beside each other. We usually had new clothes to wear on Christmas Day

After Mass we were allowed to take our presents outside to show our friends. Christmas dinner was always the best meal ever. My mother made her own puddings and Christmas cake. Sometimes we were allowed to stir the pudding mix and make a wish. My mother would put the pudding mix into clean pillowcases and hang them up to settle until Christmas Eve. The aromatic smell of spices and cinnamon would have our heads swirling with delight. After the Christmas dinner my Dad would always fall asleep in his armchair.

The Coffey's kitchen

I think my mother may have gone back to bed for an hour or so. Visitors would sometimes call to our house on Christmas night and we would most often head upstairs to our rooms to play with our toys. My brother Brendan and I would save any money we had from Christmas and walk to the shops on the New Cabra Road. There was a shop there called the Needle and Anchor that we liked to go into. They sold second-hand comics and books that we could buy quite cheaply. Between us both we would bring home quite a big collection of comics.

Christmas was such a magical time of year for all of us in number 36 Killala Road. The whole excitement and suspense of what Santa might leave filled us with delight. Everyone was in a good mood and we never really did mind all of the jobs that we had to do in preparation for the big event. It's not that I did a lot of work around the house. Like most of the others in the family I skipped out as often as I could.

Boys at play

Chapter 11

Games We Played

Boys were never as good at juggling as the girls were. My sister and her pals could juggle three tennis balls with one hand. They would throw them up against the wall in succession and not let one of them drop. Others could toss them up into the air and juggle them like a clown in the circus. Boys were just useless at anything like that. Well at least I was useless at it. The girls would sing one of several little rhymes at the same time to help them with their timing. 'One, two three O'Leary' was one of the songs they sang as they played.

The girls were also great at skipping. Again they seemed to have a better sense of timing than most of the boys. Some girls could run along the path and skip at the same time. There were certain songs they sang to help them skip in time. 'Look whose coming down the street (which ever girl was skipping would have their name mentioned at this point) with wah wah feet. She was married twenty times before now she's knocking at (a boy's name was then mentioned here) door'. Sometimes a girl skipping would get annoyed if a wrong boy's name was mentioned.

A line of girls would stand on one side of the skipping rope and one by one they would each take a turn running into the rope as it was turned and skip on through to the opposite side.

Coffey Boys 1954

If by chance one of them became entangled in the rope they then had to take a turn on the rope. 'Janie Mack my shirt is black what will I do for Sunday. Go to bed and cover your head and don't get up 'til Monday'.

Piggy Beds was a game that both boys and girls could play together. You needed an old polish tin filled with mud or muck as they called it back then. You also needed a piece of chalk. A rectangular shape was marked out on the ground and divided into eight or maybe twelve equal parts. The parts were then numbered from one to eight or to twelve. In the first instance numbers four and seven were called rest beds. There were certain rules that had to be strictly adhered to if you wanted to play. The way we played it you could only hop once in a bed. We had to decide at the beginning if 'inchies' were allowed. If you hopped and didn't land close enough to the piggy you could inch your foot forward until you got near enough to push the piggy along into the next box. After you had completed a round successfully you could pick out another rest bed for yourself. Only you were allowed to rest in it. You would then write your initials on it and everyone else in turn had to jump over it.

A favourite game of mine was 'kick the can'. We had to wait until it was dark to play this game. And again both boys and girls could play it together. To start off you needed an empty tin can. Someone had to volunteer to be 'on it'. They would then sit by the side of the road with their face hidden in their arms.

John Burke

They would hit the can against the side of the footpath as they counted to one hundred in fives. The rest of the gang would then scatter into hiding. The best place to hide was in someone's garden. The person who was on it would then have to find the hiding place of each gang member. If someone was spotted hiding then the person on it would run back to the tin can and bang it three times on the ground calling out the other person's name and place of hiding. When anyone was caught they had to sit on the ground near to the tin can. If a person in hiding was quick enough they could run out of hiding and kick the can. If the person on it could run and touch them before they kicked it then that person had to be on it. The game would start all over again.

Other games we played were the mowl, swings on the lamp-post, marbles, conkers, red rover, relievee-i-o, postman's knock and spin the bottle. A hoop was another thing that boy's mainly played with. This was the wheel off a bicycle without a tyre or tube on it. You would use a small piece of stick to push it along with. You could run along with it like a train or a stagecoach. You could even have a race with other boys. A Hoola Hoop could be used in the same way. Some girls could skip through the Hoola Hoop. The Hoola Hoop was made of plastic and was much lighter than the bicycle hoop.

Noel Coffey

Trolleys and Boxcars

Another great means of mobility was the four-wheeled trolley or boxcar. The bigger boys usually made these or someone's Dad might get involved in its creation. A long length of wood was used for the main body part. An axle was added to the back part and a steering axle was put on the front. The front axle was moved by means of a length of rope being tied to each side of it. This enabled the driver to turn the trolley to the left or to the right.

Four small steel wheels with ball bearings inside them were then attached to the end of each axle. I think these were stolen from the railway. All that the driver needed now was someone to push the trolley from behind and away he went. Other trolleys had four wheels off a baby's pram. Gangs of kids could ride on it. They were relatively easy to make and were very cost effective. Trolleys and boxcars were used for everything from keeping children amused to collecting bags of turf and the collection of items for recycling. This of course was a time before plastic bags and plastic bottles came into fashion or even recycling centres as we know them today. Very little was thrown away or wasted. Rags, bottles and jam jars were all recycled. Woolen jumpers and trousers were handed down from one brother to another until they eventually ended up as rags for cleaning and polishing the house with.

Martin, Bernard & Brendan Coffey

The Ragman

The Ragman was a popular and regular sight around the roads of Cabra West. Some of them arrived driving an ass and cart and others came pushing big wicker baskets on wheels. "Rags bottles and jam jars" they would cry. In return for old clothes they gave you a balloon on the end of a piece of bamboo stick that had coloured feathers stuck to it. Sometimes they would give you a cup and saucer. I gave my Communion suit away to a ragman. When my mother realized what I had done she ran out onto the road calling after the galloping ass and cart as it swiftly headed out of sight. I could hear bells ringing in my head for a long time afterwards.

Early Recycling

On other occasions the trolley was used for collecting old newspapers and glass bottles. Sometimes a pram was used with or without the baby in it. A group of kids would come together and go from house to house asking the owner if they had any old newspapers and bottles they didn't want. We would walk the legs off ourselves going around. This was the original era of recycling. The newspapers and bottles were put into sacks and brought to either one of two places.

Helen Coffey centre

There was a man that had a collection point in a laneway off the North Circular Road end of Blackhorse Avenue. Another collection point was off North King Street opposite Smithfield. This is where a man we knew as Harry Littleman was based. He would count out all the bottles from the sacks and then weigh the sacks of newspapers.

Sometimes the lads would have placed a couple of big heavy stones at the bottom of the sack to add weight to the papers. You were paid by the weight. There was a lot of effort involved for such little reward that had to be shared amongst a crowd of six or seven of us. Sometimes the stuff would have to be stored overnight in someone's house or backyard. After school the next day it was brought to Harry's yard.

Comics

The comics I enjoyed most as a young boy were the Beano and Dandy. The Beano had the Bash Street Kids and Dennis the Menace in it. The Dandy had Desperate Dan and his cow-pie dinners. There was also Winker Watson and Korky the Cat. In later years I preferred the Victor, the Hotspur and the Topper. I was never too keen on the Eagle, Roy of the Rovers or the Beezer.

Brendan Coffey & his Dad

My younger sisters would get the Judy and the Bunty. I loved to read the story of the Four Mary's. They were kind of private school detectives. There were cut-out dolls on the back page with little clothes to fit on them. All of these comics of course were imported into Ireland from England and we had to pay extra for them. There were also comics called sixty fourers. These were smaller comics mainly aimed at boys. They had stories of Kit Carson and Hop along Cassidy and stories of the Second World War. Swapping comics became a great past-time on winter nights.

Boys would come knocking on our door looking for swaps. We would agree to exchange comics with each other. Some comics had more value than others. The more costly comics like the American Dell comics demanded three or four Beanos in exchange for one of these types. Other times we would go calling at boys houses to swap what comics we had. I would try to find a quiet corner somewhere and settle down for a good read. A new comic would cost more in Ireland than in England. They cost three pennies in England but our local shop always charged us more. That was the reason I preferred to buy secondhand comics.

Vinnie Butler Brendan Coffey & John Burke

My First Accident

When I was four years old I was involved in an accident. The way it happened was that my father was driving home on his motorbike from work during his lunch break, which was something he often did, especially on Fridays. He would come home with his wage packet and give it to my mother so that she could buy some food to feed us all. Sometimes he would bring home an apple tart to share with my mother while they had a cup of tea. As he sped across the river Liffey northwards across Queen Street Bridge a car drove out of a side street coming from Smithfield. The car drove straight across the path of the motorbike. The front wheel of the motorbike buckled on impact and my father was hurled through the air.

He crashed in through the window of a pub and landed on the floor of the bar. The barman helped him up off the floor and gave him a drop of whiskey to steady his nerves. Later on the Garda would try to charge my father with drunken driving. Word was quickly sent to my mother about the accident. She then made arrangements I suppose with some of her neighbors to keep an eye on the house and her children. At this time my sister Mary was her baby girl and I was her youngest boy. My older brother Noel was put in charge of me and was cautioned to keep an eye on me until my mother returned home from the hospital. At the time of the accident Noel was ten years old.

126

Martin Coffey 1954

Ten-year-old boys do not generally listen very much to anything they are being told and Noel was no exception. He decided to go to the nearby cattle market with his friend. I don't remember being aware of my father's dilemma or my mother's situation. Noel later told me that he lied through his teeth in court about the accident in order to save his own skin. It seems that I was trailing behind the two boys as we crossed the main Navan/Rathoath road when a small van whisked by and caught my jacket in its wing mirror.

Noel swore in court that I was standing on the footpath, which I wasn't. He knew only too well that if he had said otherwise my mother would have dealt with him later on for not keeping a proper watch over me. It seems that I was dragged along the road for several hundred feet like a little rag doll. When I eventually dropped to the ground I had a fractured skull, a broken leg, a broken collarbone, a broken ankle and several other cuts and bruises. It took a little while for Noel and his pal to realise what had happened. When my mother returned home from visiting my father in hospital the neighbours told her not to take her coat off. I have no memory of being in hospital at this time. I know from my mother that my broken leg remained in plaster for a whole year.

Holy Communion Certificate

It was my mother who first noticed that my foot wasn't right when I was sent home from the children's hospital in Temple Street. The Doctors disagreed with her and were very dismissive of her comments on their work. My ankle had to be broken again and re-set properly to my mother's satisfaction. Only for my mother's insistence I could possibly have ended up with a permanent limp for the remainder of my life. As a result I ended up with my leg in plaster for a whole year. My father had made an entry about it in his little brown leather diary. It was a constant reminder to me over the years of my accident because my father would always show it to me when he was making a new entry.

The book had the name and address of the solicitor who dealt with the case when it was brought to court. It read 'Martin to see John F. Murtagh of Eden Quay on his 21st birthday'. My father kept all of our birth dates, times and weights along with other important information relating to our family in that book. He also wrote down the date that my sister Vera left home for England when she went away to be a nurse. Quite a few girls from Cabra West went with her at the time. Like my sister some went over never to return.

Bernard Coffey Malta 1936

Back Scratching

There was little my father loved more than a snooze in his armchair after his dinner in the evening. On one particular Friday night as my father was resting his eyes Brendan and I were poking at the fire sending sparks flying up the chimney. When my father woke up we quickly put the hot poker down onto heart of the tiled fireplace. As my father yawned and stretched he asked my mother to put her hand down the back of his shirt and scratch his back for him.

Sometimes my mother would use one of her knitting needles but this time she picked up the poker that Brendan and I had used. My father let out such a roar as the hot poker sizzled the skin on his back that everyone leapt into the air with fright. I vaguely remember Brendan giving the game away by making a dash for the door as I remained seated with a stupid grin on my face. Selected memory is a great thing because I have no recollection as to what happened next. I have no doubt however that I received enough punishment for the both of us.

Chapter 12

The Sunshine House

My father brought me into a large Georgian house in Mountjoy Square when I was about nine or ten years old. I didn't know it at the time but he had arranged for me to go to the Sunshine House in Balbriggan for a week. I had no idea why he was bringing me to the Vincent de Paul office. A couple of weeks later I was shunted off on a train from James Connolly station to Balbriggan. I had no luggage with me. The train was filled to capacity with lots of other boys.

I had no idea where I was going. No-one had explained to me what was happening. I was just sent away. Besides being in hospital this was the first time I remember sleeping in a bed on my own. There were two rows of beds lined up along the big dormitory where we slept. On our very first night we were warned about Mc Kenzie's ghost. He seemingly roamed about the house in the dark of night. This was just a ploy of course to make sure we all stayed in our beds. Some days we were brought to the beach at Laytown for a swim and a sandcastle competition. I won a wind-up Donald Duck car for building the best sandcastle. Another day we were brought to Skerries to an amusement fair. We were each handed several little blue tickets that allowed us access to the amusements. When all your tickets were gone that was it, fun over.

Concert in Balbriggan

After a walk along the beach to Bettystown we would then head back to the house for our tea and a film. Other nights there was a concert held. Some of the children would take part in the entertainment by singing or telling funny stories and jokes. I never did. The leaders were great fun. They played tricks on each other all the time. One night we were taken for a walk through a graveyard. We all expected to see Mc Kenzie's ghost appear before our very eyes. Suddenly all of the leaders disappeared on us and panic set in as we ran screaming back to the house. The following Saturday we headed back to Dublin. Although I was glad to be heading home I was a little sad at leaving the new friends I had made and the freedom we had in the countryside. I was as brown as a berry from the outdoors and sunshine.

When the train arrived in Connolly station I remember seeing my two younger sisters Anne and Mary sitting on the platform. They were about to head in the direction from which I had come. The strange thing is that nobody was there to meet me to take me home. I walked to the flats complex in Sheriff Street to my cousin Chrissie Kane and her family. She fed me and her husband Billy Dillon walked me to my bus and gave me my fare home. When I arrived home nothing was said. It was almost as if I had never gone away. I suppose with so many young children running about the house one extra face didn't make much difference. I thoroughly enjoyed my week in the Sunshine House in Balbriggan. It was my first time away from home on my own.

The Cabra Grand Picture House

The Pictures

On Saturdays my pals and I would go to the Cabra Grand picture house. It cost ten pennies to get in. We were made to queue up outside the front entrance. The usher wore a smart uniform and cap. He looked like someone from a showband. There was always pushing and shoving going on and others trying to skip the queue. If the usher got really annoyed at us he would let those at the bottom of the queue in first. On Sunday we had to queue around the side of the picture house. As soon as you would walk into the foyer area the smell of freshly made popcorn would hit you. A woman made the popcorn and I think she had a limp or bad hip.

When you got your ticket at the window you had to hand it to the attendant who tore it in half and gave you a piece back. It would take a while for your eyes to become accustomed to the lack of light. The cinema was always packed with kids. We were always shown two films and a trailer. As the big curtain was about to open a great giant seashell would appear on the screen and open up. Sometimes the Path News would be shown first. This showed a series of topical events from around the world. For some reason they always showed the Queen of England on holidays. There was never any news about Ireland or Cabra West.

Plaza Cinema Parnell Square

The usher would do his rounds and warn us all to shut up and be quiet. The small picture would come on first. It might be a cowboy film or tales from Scotland Yard. Sometime they might have a Folly–Upper that was shown in episodes on a weekly basis. This was sure to make you want to come back the next week to see what happened to the chap and his moth. They might have an interval before the big film. A girl would walk down the aisle carrying a tray in front of her that contained ice-pops, ice-cream, drinks and bags of popcorn.

Free Drinks

One thing that my pals and I would often do during the interval was to crawl under our seats looking for chewing gum that someone had thrown away. We would spit on it to make it clean and then chew on it for a while. There was always a little sweet taste still on it. Another thing that we would do while on the floor was to look for an empty ice-cream carton. We would take it down to the toilets with us, scraping out any leftover ice-cream on the way. One of us would then pull the chain hanging down from the toilet cistern. Water was then scooped up from the bowl into the container for us to drink.

The State Cinema in Phibsborough was a posh place to go to because it cost one shilling to get in. We had to queue down along the steps at the side of the building. This is where part of the Royal Canal once flowed.

Our Gang

In 1959 I went with some of my brothers and sisters to see the film Darby O'Gill and the Little People in the State Cinema. It was the first time I saw Sean Connery in a film and he was singing. If you really wanted to impress a girl you always brought her to the State Cinema. Around the corner was the Boh' or to give it its proper title the Bohemian Cinema. It was situated across the road from Phibsborough Shopping Centre. It had a very posh sounding name but it was in fact a flea pit. You might walk in but the fleas would carry you out. It was never very clean and was the cheapest priced cinema of them all. It only cost eight pennies admission.

There was always at least one queer who would sit beside you. He would offer you some sweets as he asked if the picture was long started. Then he would place his coat across his lap and have part of it on your leg. He would place his hand on your knee before beginning the ascent upwards and across. One night myself and two of my friends were barred from the Boh' because we beat the hell out of a queer for feeling my leg. The usher smashed his torch to pieces on my head. Looking back I can appreciate how dangerous these men were as they preyed on young children in the darkness of the cinema. The Bohemian was a well known haunt for this particular type of dangerous individual.

Aggie and Archie Coffey

I mostly loved the musical films with Doris Day or Elvis Presley. In later years my mother told me that my father was in love with Doris Day. He knew the words of all her songs and had seen all her films. I think I was about ten years old when I first fell in love with Haley Mills. In one film called 'Whistle down the Wind' she thought a man on the run from the police was Jesus.

When the Hollywood films came on the screen we were all lost in space. We had no idea what we were looking at. They always had perfect houses with giant gardens and two cars. The children in the American films always had their own bedrooms that were bigger than our entire house at home. It was absolute and total fantasy but I loved it.

Hearing Difficulty

One time my mother brought me to a clinic in Lord Edward Street to have my hearing tested. She was convinced that I was slightly deaf. The doctor would ring a little bell behind my left ear and then behind my right ear. He tried out a few other little tests and then looked at my mother. He told her that I had no problem hearing anything that she said and that I simply chose not to heed what she said. I knew that I was in serious trouble by the look on my mother's face.

Anne Coffey

The Messenger

Whenever my older brothers sent me to the shops they always put a note in my pocket to make sure that I didn't forget what it was I was sent for. One time they put a note in my hand to remind me of the note in my pocket. If I was ever sent to the shops by my mother for a loaf of bread I would often bring it home half eaten. There was always a fight as to who got the cats-skin. This was the side crust on the loaf. Later on sliced bread became the fashion. Our favourite bread was Batch Loaf. Another thing that happened to me was my mother sent me to the chipper window for two bottles of milk. A note in the window said' No Bottles No Milk'. Being Sunday evening meant that the window was the only shop open. At the time I didn't understand that I had to have an empty milk bottle to give in exchange for a full one. I went home and told my mother that the shop had no milk. I explained about the note in the window so she sent my brother back to the shop instead.

The Chip Shop

In later years each Friday almost every family in Cabra West lived out of Mister Cafolla's chip shop on Fassaugh Avenue. The queue would stretch for miles outside the chipper and along by the other shops. We were sent for ten or twelve bags of chips every Friday. They sold a variety of fish including smoked cod and ray. The ray was great because you could spend ages sucking on the bones.

Helen Coffey

The best thing about the chip shop was the smell of the salt and vinegar that was loaded onto every order. A plate of chips and a few slices of batch loaf was a feast in itself.

Neighborhood Characters

One time there was a woman that lived in a little house at the side entrance to Saint Joseph's School for Deaf and Dumb children on Rathoath Road. We always called her Mad Mary. She had a small dog that she had trained to attack you if you came too near to her gateway. As the dog was snapped at your heels Mad Mary would come up behind you and pull you by the hair. What a strange woman. There was also a man that lived on Rathoath Road who dressed in the clothes of a monk. One day he was found dead in the nearby canal under Broombridge. I never knew who these people were or even their names.

There was also Mrs. Donnelly that sold out-of-date fruit every Sunday morning at Drumcliffe roundabout. She would sit on the wall beside the steps leading onto the roundabout. She had her fruit displayed on a large breadboard placed on top of a baby's pram. She only charged a penny or two pence an apple. It never bothered us children whether the fruit was fresh or not we ate it either way. On an odd occasion a brass band would set up in the roundabout on Drumcliffe Road.

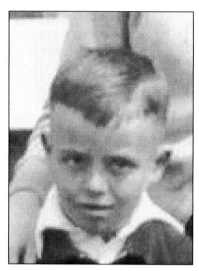

The Haircut

As the musicians tuned up their instruments gangs of young children would gather around to hear what they were going to play. Misses Mahon from Rathoath Road sold fresh fish outside our house every Friday. She would stand beside her wicker basket trolley and cut the heads off the fish. Mister Keogh that lived on the corner of Rathoath Road and Drumcliffe Road had a shop van. I remember he had a bubble gum machine standing beside it.

The Barber

A barber used to come around the area on a Saturday night. He would call to your house and ask if anyone needed a haircut. He only cut boy's hair. We never liked him coming into our house because he would always take lumps of flesh off the back of our necks. He would use one of those old fashioned hand operated gadgets. It had two handles that he would squeeze together and this mechanism caused two blades to move in opposition to each other and hopefully it would cut your hair.

When they failed to do so the barber would pull the machine away from your neck in a rapid motion. This resulted in lumps of skin being yanked off the back of your neck. The same barber came around on Sunday selling ice cream from a large box attached to the front of a tricycle.

The Blackrock

Another barber in our area would cough and spit down your neck as he was cutting your hair. He would always make me sit on a piece of wood placed across the arms of the barber's chair. After chopping my hair and neck he would splash me all over with some awful smelly water he called hair oil. A man called "Smell the bottles" would cut your hair for an empty bottle or jam jar. He would always smell the bottles first.

During the months of September and October my father would sometimes bring us up along the canal towards Ashtown to pick blackberries. We were not allowed to pick the ones near to the ground because the Devil had spit on them. If we ever managed to bring enough home my mother would make some jam with them. At the opposite end of the canal my father brought us to the football fields to collect mushrooms. When you walked over Broombridge there was a house belonging to a man named Beano in a field where all the factories are situated today.

My father remembered a ruin of a house on the corner of Fassaugh Avenue and Rathoath road that he said had once belonged to Lord Norbury. He was called the hanging judge. He was known to fall asleep in court and when he would awaken he would shout out "Hang him".

Joe Ellis. John Farrell, Jimmy Sherry & Martin Coffey

One time a goat was placed in front of him and when he woke up he screamed as usual and the goat had to be hanged. He was later responsible for hanging the Irish rebel Robert Emmett.

One time my brother Bernard and his pals brought me up along the banks of the river Liffey to the Strawberry Beds. I remember them diving off some kind of stone arch. One of the lads dived from the arch and cut his head on a rock hidden underneath the water. I had no swimming nicks of my own then so I would have to borrow a pair of knickers belonging to my older sister. I would have to tie a piece of twine around the waist to stop them from slipping down.

Ned, John, Anne, Kathleen & Baby Vera Burke

Chapter 13

The Burkes

The Burkes are our cousins. My Aunt Kathleen and her husband
Ned Burke lived on Broombridge Road. My grandmother had lived
there with them for many years. I remember my mother sending
some of us to Kathleen on a Thursday night. My uncle Ned worked
in the ESB and was paid on Thursday. Because my mother had little
or no money on Thursday we were sent to Kathleen and my Granny
to be fed our tea. My cousin John Burke often delivered turf to the
elderly people in Cabra West. When he received a cheque for this
work he always donated the money to the Old Folks Christmas
Party. He never kept a penny for himself. Kathleen and Ned have
eight children. Ned is from Tipperary.

Hospitalized

In 1963 my older sister Chrissie was married to Tony Duffy from
Inchicore. They were married in Cabra West Church. I was
supposed to be the Page Boy all dressed in white. The night before I
became quite ill and was taken to the Children's Hospital in
Crumlin. I was threatened with a burst appendix. I missed the
wedding and all of the fanfare that went with it and the grushie. I
remember a nurse Rack taking care of me.

Tony Duffy and Chrissie Coffey

Shortly after my release from hospital my mother brought myself and two of my brothers, Brendan and Tony to England on holiday. We went to an open air swimming pool there that had no filthy kids swimming in it or dead horses floating on the water. Brendan and I robbed apples from a tree that was growing in someone's front garden. Imagine having an apple tree growing in your front garden at home. The local kids would look like white maggots on a dead cat as they descended on the apples. It was so different to Cabra West and so clean. I didn't like having to wash my hands so often.

Cabra West Technical School

When I was thirteen years old I left Saint Finbarr's School. I graduated into the Cabra Technical School. I was sorry to leave Finbarr's having spent the best part of seven years there. I was sorry to leave my teacher. I took an instant dislike to the Tech. For me at that time the attitude of a few teachers towards their pupils left a lot to be desired. The one positive thing was that they were not allowed to use a cane on us as a means of punishment. In some cases I would have preferred the cane rather than have the teacher make little of me in front of the whole class.

I really had trouble with this whole issue of bullying by certain teachers. I rebelled totally against them in every way I could. This of course got me into a lot of trouble. We had a priest that went around the neighborhood with a big Alsatian dog on a lead. To me he was just as much a bully as the teachers. One time he threw a duster at me because I laughed at some story or other he was telling us.

142

Granny Burke 1964

Whack…the duster hit me full force on my forehead. Then without thinking I picked up the duster and threw it back at him. It just about missed him and crashed into the blackboard behind him. He dragged me by the neck out of the classroom and threatened to beat me up. He banned me from his class for two or three weeks. I was delighted.

Facts of Life

I loved Woodwork and Mechanical Drawing, English and Art. One day we were informed that the priest was going to talk to us individually about the facts of life. The lads were all buzzing with excitement. At last we were going to know about all those things that adults spoke about in whispers when we were around. When it came my turn I was very nervous. I walked into the room and sat on a chair opposite the priest. He asked me if I ever masturbated. I looked at him with a puzzled expression because I had never heard that expression before.

I honestly had no idea what he meant. "Do I ever what father"? He looked at me as if I was an alien. "Never mind" he said. "Just send in the next boy". One of the older boys later told me in normal language what the priest meant. Another time I was asked the same question by a Priest when I went to confession. He told me that if I did I should call to his house later that evening to discuss it with him.

The Coffey's in the 1960's

Girls Jeans

One time my mother brought me home a pair of jeans from England. They were red and had a black pinstripe down the legs. There was no fly or zip on the front of them, it was at the side. They were girl's jeans. I was given no choice. I had to wear them. I would walk to school with my books placed in front of my crotch so that nobody would notice I had no fly. Strangely enough not one boy in the school ever made any mention of it to me. One day in our Irish class Mister Smart Alec teacher asked me where I got the clown's trousers from. That finished me with his class. I got up from my seat and walked out. I never went back to studying Irish because of him. In Finbarr's school I had loved Irish. In order to avoid any further situations of confrontation with certain teachers I had my mother write a note requesting that I be excused from these classes. I was then allowed attend extra art classes.

Major Achievement

I loved the art class and the teacher we had. She was a small woman with a hump or some kind of disfigurement but she was great. I won an all Dublin Technical Schools art competition because of her. She showed great patience with me and gave me plenty of encouragement.

June, Joe & Helen Coffey

I was presented with a certificate of achievement and ten shillings for getting first place. My mother later told me that one of the people attending the awards had suggested to her that I should be sent on to Art College. My mother explained our family situation to the person. The money was never there for college with so many children in the family. There was no government grant available either at that time.

My First Guitar

At about this time I was taking guitar lessons in the Belvedere Newsboys Club in Marlborough Street. Like my father and my older brothers before me, I had joined this club when I was twelve years old. One year my older brother Brendan was given a guitar for Christmas. As it sat in our bedroom I took it up and plonked on it. To my total amazement I managed to play part of a tune on one of the strings. I played it over and over.

A few weeks later I saw a group of older boys standing on the corner of the road where I lived. One of them had a guitar and was playing it as other boys sang along with him. I ran home and grabbing Brendan's guitar darted straight back to the singing group. The group of boys asked me if I could play anything on my guitar. I sat up on the wall and placing the guitar across my knee played on one string.

Martin Coffey 1968

The whole group burst into laughter and one of the boys asked me to play a proper tune for them. I had no idea what he meant. He took the guitar from me and as he strummed it he told me it was out of tune. I had no idea at that time that a guitar had to be tuned. Along with the other guitar player he tuned the guitar for me and showed me how to hold down a chord. He sent me home and told me to practise until I had it off sound perfect. He also warned me not to touch the tuning knobs. That is how I started off on the guitar.

Every evening I would dash up the road with Brendan's guitar in hand and join the big boys for a session. They were very patient with me as I struggled with each new piece of information and lesson they gave me. I soon noticed that the tips of the fingers on my left hand were becoming raw from use on the strings. Sometimes my fingers would actually bleed. I really didn't mind as long as I was able to play a tune. Most people in the neighbourhood knew I was able to play the guitar because I would often sit on our front gate at night playing and singing to myself. Sometimes a few girls would gather around and join in. Sean Quinlan used to call me Elvis.

Career Guidance

When it came near time for me to leave the Cabra Tech two teachers came into our classroom. They were supposed to be our career guidance teachers. Each one of the boys had to stand up in front of the whole class and say what it was they would like to do after they were finished with school.

Anne, Mary, Catherine, Tony & June Coffey

One boy was planning on taking up work as a painter with his father. Another boy was going to get a job in a nearby clothing factory. When it came to my turn I stood up and said that I would like to work at art or music. This would have surprised no one of the boys in my class. They all knew what I liked to do most. Mister Smart Alec teacher looked over at me with a scowl on his face.

He told me to sit down and not to be stupid. He told us not to fool ourselves as to our future. He made some comments about my home situation and working class families. I was furious with him. Over the years I have often wondered how many young lives he was responsible for destroying through his negative attitude. The other teacher stood by and did nothing to correct the situation.

The first teacher then addressed the class and told us that we were factory fodder. We would basically work and die in a factory because that was all we deserved. He certainly seemed to have a chip on his shoulder. I fail to understand why we were never given proper career guidance. Even if we were only fit for factory work perhaps a kind word in the right direction may have helped some boy or other. I eventually left the Cabra Tech at fifteen years of age. I was none the better for the experience. Like many other boys I knew of I was glad to get away from such negative surroundings.

Martin Coffey centre back & the Belvedere Beats RTE 1967

Television Appearance

A short while later the Belvedere Newsboy's Club was approached by the State sponsored television station R.T.E. and asked if they could supply a few lads for a programme that they were putting together on youth clubs in Dublin. The immediate choice of course was the guitar class. Four guitar players, one tambourine player/singer and a drummer were selected. We were taken to a church hall on the south side of the city for the audition. The programme was to be pre-recorded. This meant that we could all sit at home and see ourselves singing and playing on television. When we arrived at the television station everyone seemed to be running about with someone shouting orders.

The set we were to play on was completely white, the stage area and the backdrop. We were given no rehearsal time. We played on our ordinary acoustic guitars and I sang for the first time into a real microphone. The feeling was electric. As I stood there playing my guitar I could watch our group on a nearby monitor. It was the greatest feeling ever. Afterwards we each received a voucher for a record shop from the stage manager. The voucher covered the cost for one single record and a little extra to which I had to put my own money to for a second record.

Martin & Brendan Coffey 1968

Great Expectations

On that Christmas Eve night my family sat around the television keen to see me on the telly. I had warned my younger sisters not to make a sound when the show aired. I did not want to miss one second of the performance. Looking back I think that every family on our road were glued to their own televisions waiting for me to appear. After the show was over some of my friends came knocking on our door for me. I remember a group of the neighbours coming to me and telling me how well I did. This went on for a while over the Christmas period and eventually phased itself out. In the Christmas edition of the R.T.E. television guide for that year a photograph of our little band was printed.

Bands and Dances

I sometimes had my band set up in our little parlour. We had two or three amplifiers, full drum kit, guitars and microphones blasting away. Our neighbours never complained about the noise. Sometimes a group of girls would gather outside on the footpath and teach each other to jive. They would knock on the parlour window and shout in requests for us to play. A dance or Hop was held in Finbarr's hall every Sunday afternoon when I was about fourteen. A fellow sat at a table up on the stage and played records. He was brutal and so were his records.

149

Billy Coffey

Later on the priest from the Tech ran a dance on Friday nights. There was live music by a group called the Sandmen. They were absolutely brilliant musicians. I would sit up at the front of the stage trying to figure what guitar chords they were playing for particular songs. The lead guitarist could always manage to get the sound of a bell from his guitar when they were singing the Beatles song Penny Lane. They had three guitar players and a drummer. I think they originally came from Swords.

You had to have a membership card to get into the Friday night dance. Sometimes the priest would patrol around the roads of Cabra West looking for any boys from the Tech. If he saw you he would confiscate your dance membership card for hanging around the street corner. I was forever being caught because I was standing there playing guitar with the bigger boys. I loved the Beatles and the Rolling Stones the most. My mother bought a set of Beatle curtains for our house. They acted as a divider between the cooking area and the eating area of our kitchen. She later cut them down to size and made them into armchair covers. My older brother Bernard went to see the Rolling Stones as well as all the top groups and acts that came to a Dublin stage. One of my friends introduced me to the music of John Mayall. It was a life changing moment for me. I was hooked on the Blues. There was always some kind of music in our house with my father singing in the bathroom and records blaring out the latest in pop music. Strangely enough I never heard my mother singing.

Kennan's Ironworks Fishamble Street

Chapter 14

Working Life

When I finally left school my father wanted me to go into an apprenticeship. The very thought of being tied down to the same job and in the same factory for the rest of my working life had no appeal to me. There was no work on offer in the music or art world either so I took on a job in a sewing machine factory. The previous summer I had worked my school holidays with Brother Sewing Machines in Santry. I was paid four pounds a week. My job then was to put an electric plug on each machine as it came along the assembly line. So here I was back where I started and being paid five pounds a week. This time around I worked in the paint spraying room.

Of course I got the usual run around because I was new at the job. I was sent to fetch a long wait and a tin of striped paint amongst other things. It was all part of ones initiation into the world of adult males. I enjoyed working there until most of the work force was made redundant just before Christmas of that year of 1967. My brother Brendan worked in the factory next door so we would travel to work together each morning. One night I decided to go to bed early so that I would have plenty of time the next morning for a good breakfast before heading off to work.

Bernard & Paddy Coffey with Ned Burke

At some stage Brendan woke me up to tell me that we were late for work. Without question I jumped out of bed and scrambled to get myself dressed and out the door. My father kept calling to me. I was in a crazy hurry, what was he wanting to delay me for. When I eventually went to his room like a raving lunatic he asked me what time it was. I looked at my watch and saw that it was eleven o'clock night time. Brendan was hiding under his bedclothes waiting for my punches to rain down on him. No matter how hard I pounded him he just laughed all the more. I was awake most of the night.

House Fire

In August of 1967 my mother and family all headed off on holiday to stay with my married sister Vera in England. The only people left at home were my Dad and I. On her departure my Dad had promised my mother that he would redecorate the kitchen/dining room for her while she was away. This was the 1960's and a time of total revolution on all things from the past. The fashion for house décor was venetian blinds, tiled fireplaces and plastic everything. This included lampshades, tiles, curtains and table clothes. Modernity had come to rule in the Dublin suburbs. On this particular day the area my Dad had painted and decorated looked really well. There were new blue and white plastic tiles on the wall around the cooker and new wallpaper was put up on the walls and ceiling. The woodwork was all painted anew. Everything looked so bright and new.

Joseph Coffey

It seemed a glorious summer to a young fifteen year old. Procol Harem was number one in the charts with "Whiter Shade of Pale". I was working in my first job with Brother International Sewing Machines in Santry and had money in my pocket. My first job initially involved putting one electric plug onto each sewing machine as it came along the production line. After a few weeks I was upgraded to the Paint Spray-Room where scratched or damaged sewing machines were re-sprayed and heat-treated. I was in love with life. I could afford to buy myself new clothes. One of the first shirts I bought myself was tangerine in colour and had a button-on frill down the front with frills on the cuffs. This was my stage shirt. On this particular day I was hurriedly cycling home from Santry because I was playing my guitar in a band later that evening. I was anxious to go over the songs that had been arranged for the band to play. I wanted to have everything off chord perfect.

As I cycled over Cardiffbridge in Finglas a sun-shower burst open and I was given quite a soaking. As I arrived at my home I noticed some workmen standing outside the gate of our house. They advised me to fill up a kettle of water because they were in the process of turning the water off in order to carry out some repair or other. I dashed into the house and not only did I fill the kettle full of water but I also managed to fill a basin that was in the kitchen sink.

The Men's Labour Exchange Gardiner Street

My clothes were damp from the rain and I needed to change into something dry. I was also hungry and in need of a dinner. I decided to make myself some chips and so I put on the chip-pan to heat up while I slipped upstairs to change my clothes. When I had changed into dry clothes I decided to pick up my guitar and practice a few numbers. I always stood in front of the bedroom mirror to practise how I would look. After a while I realised that there was a strange smell coming into the bedroom. It suddenly dawned on me that I had left the chip-pan heating on the cooker.

In a blind panic I dropped my guitar onto the bed and cleared the stairs in two leaps. When I opened the kitchen door I was immediately hit with the stench of burning cooking fat mixed with the smell of melting plastic and a cloud of billowing black smoke. The chip-pan was blazing and shooting flames up the wall and straight across the ceiling into the centre of the room. The plastic lampshade was melting with the heat and dripping onto the oilcloth that was covering the table below. The plastic wall tiles were curled and melting off the wall behind the cooker. My mind was in total panic.

I snatched the flaming chip-pan off the cooker and opening the backdoor I threw it outside. As it hurled through the air some of the burning grease splashed out and ignited the curtain hanging on the backdoor. I quickly grabbed the basin of water out of the sink and doused out some of the flames. Eventually I managed to get everything under control.

Eddie Burke

The next-door neighbours and a few other neighbours came running in to see what had happened. They had seen smoke billowing out of the back of the house. All that was going through my mind was that my Dad would kill me when he found out. Here was all his hard work destroyed because of my guitar. Some neighbours took me into their house to clean myself up and then fed me a dinner. Later on the neighbours told my Dad that for the duration of my mother's holiday they would feed me a dinner each evening. I was banned forever more from cooking in my parent's home.

I was never allowed to forget this day for the remainder of my parent's lives. My father was of course livid at me when he saw the damage I had caused. His only comment in anger was to say to me ***"That bloody guitar…"*** Luckily for me he had some wallpaper and tiles left over from the original job. We both stayed up until the early hours of the morning and re-decorated the room. As we were pasting wallpaper on the ceiling my older brother's girlfriend called by to the house.

She was planning a trip over to my brother in England and she would also see my mother. My father swore her to secrecy. Nothing was to be mentioned about Martin setting fire to the house. My father told her that under no circumstances was she to say a word of what had happened to my mother. My mother was not too keen in the first place to leave me at home. I had insisted that I was too busy with my job and guitar to go on holiday. My father backed me up as my mother reluctantly agreed.

Fassaugh Avenue Shops

My Dad knew that if my mother found out about the fire from anyone other than himself that he would get it in the neck. The cover-up was perfect with the neighbours too involved in the silence of my arson attack on our kitchen.

The week following the fire my father headed off to join my mother and the rest of the family in England. He felt secure in the knowledge that word had not leaked out across the Irish Sea to my mother. As he was stepping off the train with expectations of my mother and the kids running up to him and throwing their arms around him, all hell broke loose. My mother gave him a tongue-lashing. He tried his best to play down the fire damage but to no avail. He was livid of course and tried his best to defend his decision to leave me at home on my own.

A Little Boy Drowned

On top of this story he also had to tell her of another serious incident that had happened with me back in Dublin. I think the fire had happened on a Tuesday so it would be the following Saturday that the second incident happened. On Saturday morning my Dad had planned to do some extra work for one of his fellow bank employees. As was his habit he headed off bright and early on his bicycle that morning. At around ten o'clock I headed into town with two of my friends. I think they were Tony Norton and Georgie Mc Cluskey. I had money in my pocket and I had plans to buy myself some new mod clothes. The fashion style at the time was bell-bottomed trousers and a mix of black and white with a bit of hippy thrown in for good measure.

156

Anne & Bernard Coffey

Not wanting to be outdone I bought myself a pair of black suede Beatle boots. These were basically ankle boots with a high heel on them and a zip up the side. I also bought a pair of black corduroy trousers with a jacket to match. To finish off the outfit I bought a black shirt and broad white silk necktie. I also had a small rose stuck in the lapel of my new jacket. I was dressed to kill as I headed into town later that evening with my two pals.

We were strolling through Stephen's Green chatting about music and girls. Suddenly we heard a woman screaming. We looked at each other and laughed as we thought it was a hippy woman tripping off in a Yellow Submarine. As we rounded a bend of shrubbery we saw a woman standing near to the duck pond screaming at the top of her voice.

I noticed that there were other people sitting nearby on the grass. Everyone seemed to be ignoring the woman's cries. She was respectably dressed and her screams sounded to me as if she was saying, "he is dead". Out of the corner of my eye I noticed something unusual floating out on the pond. It was a very young child lying face down in the water. He was out quite a distance. I was unable to swim but I never hesitated in running and jumping straight into the water. I had no idea of its depth. Without really thinking about the consequences or the possible danger to my own life I waded out to the child. I picked up the lifeless body of a little boy no older than two or three years old. He appeared to be dead.

Bernard Coffey & Mary Skelly

I looked back over my shoulder to see where my friends were and saw that a group of people had gathered on the waters edge next to the child's mother. With the little lifeless body held securely in my arms I pushed through the green slime covered water towards the waiting crowd. Everyone was reaching out their arms to help me out of the water.

Unknown to me there is a cemented incline under the water at the ponds edge. It was covered in a slimy substance and my feet slipped. I went under the water with the little boy in my arms. I banged my forehead on the cement and came up out of the water with blood streaming down my face. I must have looked a sight. A man was first to take the little body out of my arms as my two friends helped me out of the water. The man that took the boy was holding him upside down by the feet. Water was dribbling out of the mouth of the little boy. I remembered learning a little about life saving in school

I lay the boy down on his back in the grass and as best I could I applied the kiss of life to him. I am glad to say that within a short while much to everyone's relief the boy let out a very loud and gurgled scream. He was alive and I was relieved. I sat down on the grass nearby and took off my new suede boots. They were ruined as water poured out of them. All of my clothing was covered in green slime from the duck pond. A woman came over to me and handed me her headscarf to dry my feet with.

Anne Coffey

I turned around to make sure that the little boy was still alive and saw that both he and his mother had gone. There was no trace of them to be seen. My immediate thought was that the child would need medical attention. Some of the people in the crowd came over and thanked me for saving the little boy. The park attendant was in the process of closing up the park for the night. He approached the crowd of people and mistakenly thought that I had jumped into the water as a joke.

He started on at me about being a little vandal when one of my friends took him aside by the neck and told him the real story. He suggested that I go to the nearby hospital and ask the porter to dry my clothes by the hospital boiler. It was a warm August evening and the boiler was not in operation. My two friends and I walked down to O'Connell Street and hopped on a bus for home. The bus conductor came to collect our fares and asked what had happened to me.

When my friends told him the story he let us travel home free of charge. When my Dad arrived home I told him the whole story. He advised me to keep a lookout in the evening newspapers, as there was sure to be a reward offered to me for saving the little boy's life. I gave up looking after about three months. All of my new clothes were totally destroyed. My Dad gave me some money towards replacing them.

Martin Coffey 1966

Flower Power

1967 was the year of the Hippy Movement in Ireland. It was the time of Flower Power and Free Love except my friends and I never knew where to go for all this free love. We would some times go dancing to the Go Go or the Ierne or some local venue like Finbarr's Hall. I much preferred to listen to a live group rather than listen to some Disc Jockey playing scratchy records. I wore bell-bottomed trousers from O'Connor's in Abbey Street and shirts from Even Steven's in Capel Street. That was my favourite shop because it had a giant psychedelic painting on the front wall of the shop.

Scott McKenzie had a song in the charts about flowers in your hair and San Francisco. I hadn't a clue where San Francisco was. It could have been on the other side of the Liberties for all I knew. It certainly wasn't in Cabra West. All the girls started wearing mini skirts. The Parish Priest would give out about them from the pulpit at Mass. Me and my pals didn't give out about them.

We thought the girls looked great in them and especially the fishnet tights they started wearing then. Some of the lads even backcombed their hair. Well I did anyway and I thought I looked brilliant. The Honda 50 was all the rage with fellas that had a good job and could afford to pay the Hire Purchase on them. My pals and I made up our own bikes then from bits and pieces that we found.

David Duffy & Joseph Coffey

We would go into Woolworth's in Henry Street on Saturday morning and rob tins of coloured spray paint and rolls of coloured tape to make the bikes look great. We would cycle out to Bray on Sunday morning and spend the day there checking out the talent.

We would cycle out along by Ringsend and Sandymount singing our heads off and laughing at anything and anyone that we passed by. My Dad worked in a kiosk on the seafront during the summer. Someone he knew from Camden Street ran it. He would always give us loads of sweets and a bottle of lemonade each. There was a cable car that went part of the way up Bray Head. One time we went up on it and threw stones down at the courting couples lying in the grass below.

It was a time of innocence for us young lads. We had no worries and the world was our oyster. What a pity we didn't realise it at the time. We cycled all over the Phoenix Park and out through Castleknock to the countryside. Sometimes we would cycle to the seaside resorts of Malahide and Portmarnock on the north side of Dublin. We would spend our time skimming stones on the water and jump them over the waves that came rolling in from the Irish Sea.

Crean's Soap Factory Dublin

Chapter 15

Job Experiences

I went to work in a pram factory in Santry. On of the men I worked with showed me a photograph of a naked girl. At first I was unsure as to what I was looking at because of the angle from which the photograph was taken. I thought it was a dog without a tail. After the man explained it to me I pretended that I knew all along what I was looking at. I left the pram factory and went to work in a brush factory near Bolton Street. I only lasted three days there because the woman was too bossy. Jobs were relatively easy to come by back then but the pay was cheap.

I started working in Kennan's ironworks in Fishamble Street. This was located on the site of the original theatre where the German composer George Handel first played his famous Messiah and the Hallelujah Chorus. The first performance took place in Fishamble Street on the 13th April 1742. Under the window of the front office a plaque was placed commemorating Handel's performance. When I first went in through the doorway of the ironworks I saw two or three different levels of work areas that looked like the inside of a theatre. There was also access to an upper level nearer to the roof of the building.

Helen Coffey

Kennan's made everything from metal stairways to railings and steel building girders. I was often sent out on a job with one of the welders. We worked in the Top Hat ballroom in Bray installing a staircase and in the vault of a bank in Thomas Street where I wrote my name in chalk behind a part of the vault. I always came home filthy dirty from this job. I would have to scrub the dirt off myself any night I was to go out and play with a group.

Music Venues

When I was about fourteen I saw an advertisement in the evening paper asking for people with musical talent to join a variety group. I showed it to my father and he encouraged me to write off about it. I received a prompt reply by post and was invited to an audition the following Friday night at an address in Parnell Square. The auditions were held in a large room filled with all sorts of musicians and acts.

When it came my turn I was very nervous so I belted out a couple of songs and played my guitar. I met a few lads from Crumlin who called themselves 'The Cooley Folk'. Within a week I received the good news telling me that I had passed the audition. It so happened that everyone else had passed it too. We played in a great variety of places from hospitals to Old Folks Homes to Schools. I loved every minute of it and practised in front of the bedroom mirror every night.

163

Bernard Coffey with Mona and Molly O'Brien

I also played with a group of lads from Sheriff Street. Our drummer was called Geronimo because he had long hair down to his waist and he resembled the character we had seen on the cowboy and Indian films. One Saturday night we were due to play in a pub called the Railway Bar in the Sheriff Street area. When I arrived with guitar in hand I was unable to find the pub. I knew it had been there the night before because we had played in it. All that was left of the pub was an empty space of charred and smoking timbers.

Someone had set it on fire shortly after we had left the night before. We played in Noctor's pub around the corner instead. An odd time I was asked to play with a group in Barry's Hotel. We played for the interval and were never paid a penny. On both sides of the dance hall there were mirrors reaching from one end of the hall to the other. The lads were on one side of the hall eyeing up the talent across the floor. We had the same arrangement with the Eurovision Club in Mountjoy Square. I played in a lot of places but was seldom paid. We were often told it was great experience for us.

On the rare Sunday afternoon I played in Saint Finbarr's Hall in Cabra West. In the late 1960's the Mater Dei Youth Club asked me to play the guitar for them in a talent competition. We practised three songs including the Beach Boy's number Sloop John B for about three weeks. With a little bit of harmony thrown in we sounded pretty good. We travelled by bus to the South Circular Road. The number twenty-two bus went straight from Fassaugh Avenue to the venue we were playing at.

Bernard Coffey wearing a cap

We came first of course and won the competition. In the late 1960's I began working for Sanbra Fyffe in Santry. They produced plumbers' fittings by the thousands. I worked in the stores helping the older men with orders for local plumbing businesses. The company supplied most of the fittings for the new Ballymun housing complex. In late 1970 I was nineteen years old and married. The time had finally come for me to say goodbye to Cabra West and Ireland.

I took the cattle boat and sailed across the water to England. I went to live with my older brother Bernard and his family in the south of England. I was never again to return to Cabra West to live. I would of course visit with my parents and family that still lived there. After a couple of years in England I returned to Dublin and worked in Crean's Soap Factory in North King Street. Then I moved to Waterford where I lived for almost ten years. I eventually returned to Dublin in the 1980's.

Since living outside of Cabra West for such a long period of time I have come to appreciate and admire those people that took it upon themselves to tame and populate this area of wilderness. It was by no means an easy task for young families to take on. These are my memories of the time I spent in Cabra West. I enjoy looking back on them and reminiscing about each one. I hope that others may be inspired by what I have put together and will attempt to record their own memories of what happened all those years ago.

Aggie and Bernard Coffey

Conclusion

In August of 1989 my father passed away after a short illness. His passing left a void that could never be filled. My mother followed in the year of the new millennium 2000. She too died in August of that year. The end of an era had come. No more would we hear my father singing as he shaved in the bathroom. Never again would my mother head off with her pals to bingo in the Cabra Grand. In 1995 I recorded my mother speaking of her childhood years. For some reason I never took the opportunity to do the same with my father. I always expected my parents would live forever. On each occasion both my parents were brought to our family home and laid out for their wake. My father and mother were both cremated and now share a grave with her mother in Glasnevin cemetery.

My youngest brother Joseph passed away on Friday 13th January 2006. The family home was eventually sold to a young couple. Once again the sound of little children's cries and singing could be heard throughout the house were so many of the Coffey children had once freely played. For over half a century the Coffey family has lived and continues to live in Cabra West. Growing up in such a large family was never easy but it was a great learning experience. It gave me a good grounding in survival skills that have always stood me well in life. How my parents lived to the age that they did is a miracle in itself. The hardship and worries that plagued them for years would put most modern day parents into an early grave.

Tenements from Waterford Street

Like fleas and hoppers that feasted on us daily the days of extra large families struggling as my parents did is almost a thing of the past. My children's children will never have to experience the settling of DDT dust into their lungs or the constant battle over a coat on their bed every night. Life has become a little easier and more settled in that sense. A museum in England dismantled the downstairs area of a local authority terraced house that was due to be demolished and re-erected it inside their museum for posterity. Liverpool city museum have also preserved items rescued from demolished local authority housing and placed them on display in their museum. They have a gallery of photographs showing the streets and houses of working class Liverpool. In my opinion the culture and environs of early Cabra West should also be remembered in this way. This may become a forgotten period of the social history of the people who had to endure so much with so little.

My people, your people and other families like them formed the very backbone of Irish society. They deserve to be remembered, recorded and honoured. Throughout my years of national schooling I was very much indoctrinated with great Irish heroes such as Pearse or Connolly but now I ask about the everyday heroes like my father and mother and all their neighbours who held this country together. Where is the recognition that they deserve? They came, they saw and they conquered a wilderness with nothing other than their bare hands and large families. In my estimation these are the real heroes.

167

My grandparents Christina and William Coffey

Basic family values in Ireland have changed very little since my childhood days. In general poverty no longer has a strangle hold on the majority of people. A greater emphasis is now placed on education and the use of modern technology in our lives. Through the use of instant internet communication it is easier to keep in touch with family members that may have emigrated. Family stories and photographs can now be recorded and stored on disc for future generations to enjoy. So I would encourage each and every family to do what they can to preserve their family heritage and to take a certain amount of pride in the achievements of those that have gone before them.

Coffey Christmas

Do You Remember Christmas?
(Martin Coffey)

Do you remember Christmas Time?
In our house years ago.
When me Da' brought home a Christmas tree
On his bicycle in the snow.

We took down the decorations
That were stored in a biscuit box
And underneath the Christmas tree
We placed our little socks.

Mammy made the puddings
In a pillowcase to hang.
While Daddy fixed the fairy lights
That were sure to make a bang.

Joseph Coffey & the Beatles Curtain

He'd either crossed a wire or two
Or hadn't got them fused.
But either way he didn't mind
It kept us kids amused.

The house was scrubbed all over
The bedrooms and the hall
The skirting boards were dusted
New paper on the wall

Everything was shining
With nothing left undone
We'd crawl upstairs exhausted
Only fit for bed each one

My sisters and my mother
Took charge to wash us clean
Into the kitchen sink we'd climb
And come out with a glean

A blazing fire was ready
Each one of us to dry
We'd gaze up at the Christmas tree
Each little girl and boy

Christmas Cowboy

Then off to bed they'd send us
But we could never sleep
The excitement was too much for us
Through the keyhole we would peep

Someone in the attic
Was handing down some toys
It wasn't Father Christmas
But Daddy in disguise

Then early Christmas morning
Down stairs we all would creep
Filled with excitement we would try
To leave our parents sleep

All around the Christmas tree
Our toys were laid out so
Scooters and prams, a cowboy suit
New pennies all aglow

Paddy Coffey 1905-1989

An orange in our stockings
With other little toys
Clockwork trains and wooden dolls
For all us girls and boys

Santa Clause had surely come
As our parents love did show
Do you remember Christmas time
In our house years ago?

Golden Wedding Anniversary 1988

Death of My Irish Parents
(Martin Coffey)

You are both gone forever never to return,
Never to travel this road again.
We can still see your footsteps in the sands of time
A forever reminder to so many little chickens
Left behind without a wing to shelter beneath.

Each one is suffering in their own private Gethsemane,
An agony of loss and displacement. Orphaned.
No more to hear the rugged words of our father's encouragement
As we stumble through life.
Or the gentle touch of our mother's hand
As she soothes our knees from when we fell.

Our eyes are burning embers of coal
Unquenched by streams of endless tears
Running down our faces like the lashing rain
On the kitchen window in those far off days
When we sat around the winter's fireside.

Safe and secure in the love which you bathed us in
Every Saturday night in preparation for Sunday Mass.
On the alter of life you sacrificed your all to pay
The price of a secure and happy home.

173

Mary Agnes Coffey

From humble beginnings you both came
And never turned away a hungry mouth or empty pocket.
Grateful we are and forever will be for bringing us
Into this world.

For breathing life into fifteen little souls
Who stand with mouths agape
Crying for sustenance from your breast.
Crying, crying, crying.

Bernard Coffey 1912 – 1989

The Day My Hero Died
(Martin Coffey)

I remember very well the time
My father passed away.
It seemed as though the world stood still,
encased in Potters' Clay.
I wanted to awaken from this nightmare
filled with screams,
To realize that this was just
another of my dreams.
Alas alas 'twas not to be.
With heartstrings torn apart
I cried and cried while wracked with pain
that split in two my heart.
I curse you God for what you've done
to cause this grief and pain.
This noble man, this Prince of Tides,
I'll never see again.

The Coffey's in Colchester, Essex

What right had you to take away
My Daddy big and strong.
I curse you still this very day
for what you did was wrong.
I barely got to say goodbye,
to give him one last kiss.
I'm still a little boy you know,
My Daddy I still miss.

THE
NEW PROGRESS
ARITHMETICS

BOOK 2

By JOHN D. SHERIDAN, M.A.

THE EDUCATIONAL COMPANY OF IRELAND, LIMITED

New Progress Arithmetics School Book

NEW
PROGRESS ARITHMETICS

BOOK 2

Revision Exercise A

Work these *Addition* sums:

(1) Hats	(2) Caps	(3) Horses	(4) Toys	(5) Pens	(6) Beans
25	37	54	35	23	16
42	27	29	46	48	26

(7) Men	(8) Women	(9) Boys	(10) Girls	(11) People	(12) Men
27	15	17	24	22	14
15	34	26	25	19	23
26	19	34	23	42	18

(13) Nibs	(14) Pens	(15) Books	(16) Cars	(17) Boats	(18) Boys
23	23	28	24	46	19
14	37	19	34	17	13
16	17	11	26	15	16

(19) s. d.	(20) s. d.	(21) s. d.	(22) s. d.	(23) s. d.	(24) s. d.
2 1	2 4	1 8	1 5	2 5	1 3
1 2	1 7	2 2	1 3	1 6	2 4

1

The New Progress Arithmetics Book 2 1958

Exercise 28
PARTS OF A POUND

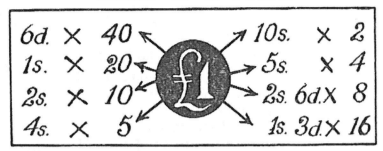

Write down the answers to these questions :

(1) How many sixpenny books can I buy for £1 ?

(2) What do **39** sixpenny tickets cost ?

(3) What is ¼ of £1 ?

(4) **8** boys share £1 equally amongst them. How much does each get ?

(5) What is ½ of **2s. 6d.** ?

(6) Cost of **8** lbs. butter at **2s. 6d.** a lb.

(7) (*a*) **4s.** × **5** ; (*b*) **5s.** × **4.**

(8) What is ½ of **5s.** ?

(9) What part of **5s.** is **1s. 3d.** ?

(10) How many tickets at **1s. 3d.** each could I buy for £1 ?

(11) (*a*) **10s.** × **2** ; (*b*) **2s.** × **10.**

(12) How many sixpences in **2s. 6d.** ?

(13) How many sixpences in **11s. 6d.** ?

(14) Find the cost of **41** sixpenny tickets.

(15) Take ½ of **5s.** from ½ of **7s.**

(16) How many half-crowns in **10s.** ?

(17) How many half-crowns in **12s. 6d.** ?

(18) How many half-crowns in **15s.** ?

(19) How many shillings in £1 **10s.** ?

(20) Express **32** half-crowns in pounds.

Pounds, Shillings & Pence 1958

THE MODEL ARITHMETIC

BOOK III

R. J. McNALLY, B.A.

BROWNE AND NOLAN LIMITED
DUBLIN   BELFAST   CORK

The Model Arithmetic School Book

REVISION EXERCISES

A

(1) **568 + 73 + 354 + 239 + 87.**

(2) There are **240** pence in a pound (£1). How many pence in £7 **10**s. ?

(3) A boy ran round this field twice.

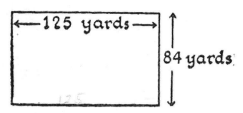

How many yards did he run ?

(4) Multiply the sum of **128** and **96** by **5.**

B

(1) If a man is **68** years of age this year, in what year was he born ?

(2) A farmer sold his land for £**4,375.** He paid £**5,500** for it a few years ago. How much money did he lose ?

(3) By how much is ⅓ of **879** greater than ⅛ of **876** ?

(4) I spent **9**s. **4½**d. on stamps, **2**s. **3**d. on a parcel and **5**s. **7½**d. on a postal order. What change did I get out of a pound note ?

Revisions Exercises

181

YOUNG IRELAND READER

PREPARATORY BOOK

BROWNE AND NOLAN LIMITED

Young Ireland Reader Preparatory Book

AM I READY FOR SCHOOL?

Is my face clean ?
Is my neck clean ?
Are my ears clean ?
Are my knees clean ?
Have I brushed my hair ?
Have I cleaned my teeth ?
Have I washed my hands ?
Am I neat and tidy ?
Have I cleaned my shoes ?
Have I a clean handkerchief ?

If the answer to all these questions is "Yes," then I am ready for school.

5

Am I Ready For School?

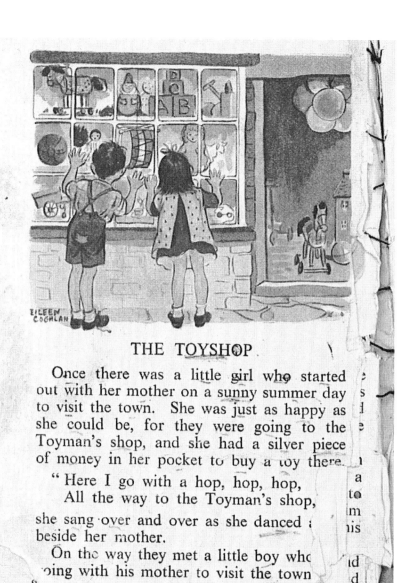

THE TOYSHOP.

Once there was a little girl who started
out with her mother on a sunny summer day
to visit the town. She was just as happy as
she could be, for they were going to the
Toyman's shop, and she had a silver piece
of money in her pocket to buy a toy there.

" Here I go with a hop, hop, hop,
   All the way to the Toyman's shop,
she sang over and over as she danced
beside her mother.

On the way they met a little boy who
oing with his mother to visit the town
g

26

The Toyshop

Young Ireland Reader Senior Book

Old Irish Coinage

Irish Half Crown

Two Shillings

One Shilling

Six Penny Bit

Old Irish Coinage

Three Penny Piece

One Penny

Half Penny

Farthing

Ms. Kathleen Atkinson
219 Ratoath Road
Cabra West
DUBLIN 7
EIRE

Thanks. Liam for all your
Help over the years!
and all the help you
gave me with the & could
Computer. Sorry classes.
not get to your
K. A.